Rebound 1983

A HANDBOOK
FOR
ELEMENTARY
SCHOOL TEACHERS

A HANDBOOK
FOR
ELEMENTARY
SCHOOL TEACHERS

Kenneth H. Hoover
Arizona State University

Paul M. Hollingsworth
University of Nevada

Allyn and Bacon, Inc.   Boston

To our mothers,

two great teachers

CONTENTS

PREFACE

Instructional processes are the tools of the teacher's trade. Without them, there is no teaching. Although all individuals—especially parents—employ various instructional procedures from time to time, it is the schoolteacher who is expected to master the art of teaching.

In addition to an adequate academic background, every beginning teacher must possess some knowledge of instructional technology. Teaching skill is developed gradually from practical experience. Strangely enough, however, the developing teacher frequently has no place to turn for assistance. As he tries methods and techniques which are new to him, he needs an easy-to-use professional reference. This is the basic purpose of this book.

A *Handbook for Elementary School Teachers* provides a basic framework for a number of instructional procedures. It offers a flexible structure from which each teacher may develop his own unique instructional skills. The techniques and methods described in this handbook are applicable to the open-school concept, the ungraded school, the British Primary School model, and the departmentalized school or the self-contained classroom. The degree of emphasis from one technique or method to another will vary depending upon the organizational structure of the school. If the British Primary School model is used, the children will be more responsible for the curriculum planned through cooperative actions. The wide variety of illustrations will enable the teacher to perfect a number of instructional techniques.

The various instructional methods and techniques described in this book are designed to be developed within a broad framework of reflective thought, each method emphasizing certain thought processes. However, full concept attainment may not be realized unless individual techniques are supplemented with other instructional techniques. Therefore, the treatment of each technique contains many cross-references to related techniques.

In the interest of practical simplicity, little effort is made to provide a full theoretical basis for the methods included. Likewise, relatively little emphasis has been placed on the specific psychological basis for each method. The framework offered in this book is fully consistent with sound psychological principles. It is assumed that the experienced teacher is reasonably well grounded in these areas. For a full treatment of both theoretical and psychological bases of instruction, the reader is referred to *Learning and Teaching in the Elementary School* (Allyn and Bacon, Inc., 1970) by the authors.

K.H.H.
P.M.H.

1

GAINING THE CONCEPT

The mental images that we carry around in our heads are known as concepts. A *concept is a mental picture of an object, event or relationship derived from experience*. Concepts help us classify or analyze; they help us associate or combine as well. These mental images gain meaning from subsequent experiences. As meaning becomes firmly established, we develop *feelings* about an idea or concept.

In the educative process, concepts are thought to form the basic *structure* of content areas. An understanding of the structural dimensions of a field of knowledge provides the learner with a frame of reference for thinking and for evaluating future experiences.

The structural properties of each teaching unit normally consist of several major concepts. These are the basic ideas which provide the focal point of instructional activities. Unit goals are derived from such concepts.

Concepts are derived from content and usually are formulated as brief, concise statements. In essence, they are the basic ideas which hold a unit together. Thus the first step in unit planning is identification of the basic unit concepts (ideas) to be sought. To illustrate from a unit in science:

1. Young plants will be almost like their parent plants.
2. Most plants have roots, stems, leaves, flowers, seeds, or fruit.
3. Seeds will grow into plants.
4. Some plant seeds and fruits are eaten by people.
5. The roots, stems, or leaves of various plants are used for food.

1

FUNDAMENTAL PROPERTIES

Concepts exist at many different levels, ranging from highly abstract symbols to complex generalizations. They are also of different types. The specific level and type to be sought is dependent upon the nature of the content area to be studied.

Concept Levels

The recent expansion of knowledge has focused attention on the importance of analysis, generalization, and application of knowledge. Rather than emphasizing specific content materials as ends in themselves, teachers have attempted to guide pupils in the reduction of content learnings to basic ideas which, in turn, can be expanded or generalized to a wide variety of problems and situations. Three distinct concept levels are necessary for such an instructional approach.

Unit Themes. At the most abstract level are unit themes (concepts), which usually are incorporated in the unit titles in such a manner as to provide direction for unit planning. Each instructional unit is based upon one such theme. For many years teachers struggled with subject-matter units, activity units, process units, and the like with relatively little satisfaction. Unit themes seem to provide the necessary cohesion and direction long sought by those who would make learning most realistic. Instead of a unit on Western Pioneers, for example, a worthwhile unit theme might be *resourcefulness.* As Chase and Howard point out, such a unit would begin with a study of contemporary issues of vital concern to youngsters.[1] For example, stress would be placed upon development of concepts of being resourceful if lost in the city or forest. Pioneers would provide a basic content reference; indeed the unit could appropriately culminate with an intensive study of Western Pioneers. Instead of a unit on the Fireman, a unit theme may be developed around the basic theme of how all workers depend upon one another in the community. Thus content emphasis is shifted from subject matter as an end in itself to its appropriate place as a means to attainment of more basic learnings.

Unit Concepts. Each unit theme, in turn, is broken into four to eight concepts, as previously described and illustrated. Often these refer to the

---

[1] John B. Chase, Jr., and James Lee Howard, "Changing Concepts of Unit Teaching," *The High School Journal* 47, no. 4 (February 1964): 180–187.

structural properties of a unit and provide the basis for derivation of unit goals.

Lesson Generalizations. As will be indicated in Chapter 2, anticipated unit outcomes provide an instructional basis for development of specific lessons. Each lesson culminates in the derivation of a number of important generalizations (concepts). Thus, unit concepts are achieved finally as pupils generalize from specific lesson activities. To illustrate from the lesson plan presented in Chapter 9 (Discussion Methods):

1. Poor diets can affect a person's health.
2. Nutritious foods help an individual to grow and develop properly.

Concept Types

The specific nature of concepts is dependent upon the nature of the unit under investigation. Pella has identified three basic types.[2]

Classificational. This is the most common concept type germane to classroom instruction. Basically its function is to define, describe or clarify essential properties of phenomena, processes or events. It is based upon the classification of facts into organized schemes or patterns. The illustrations presented in the first section of this chapter are of this type. To further illustrate in the area of science: An insect is an animal with six legs and three body cavities. Thus certain facts or observations are organized to *describe* certain phenomena in the world of reality.

Correlational. This type of concept is derived from *relating* specific events or observations; it consists of prediction. According to Pella it consists of the formulation of general principles. To illustrate in the area of science: If limestone is placed under great heat and pressure, it becomes a harder rock called marble. It will be noted that the concept consists of an *if . . . then* dimension. A *relationship* between two variables is involved.

Theoretical. A theoretical concept facilitates the explanation of data or events into organized systems. It involves the process of advancing from the known to the unknown. For example: Everything on earth is changing all the time. Even rocks must be changing. A theoretical concept goes beyond the facts, but it must be consistent with the known facts.

[2] Milton O. Pella, "Concept Learning in Science," *The Science Teacher* 33, no. 9 (December 1966): 31–34.

CONCEPT ATTAINMENT

Concepts cannot be passed directly from teacher to pupil. Prior to the educational experience, however, the teacher himself must identify essential unit concepts. They, in turn, become the structural bases for development of necessary learning activities. Concepts are derived from the processes of reflection. Thus instructional experiences must be conceived within such a framework. The nature of the concept being sought will determine which of the various steps of the reflective or cognitive process will be stressed.

The Problem

A problem arises when an individual encounters difficulty in his regular activities. He recognizes that the concepts at hand somehow do not fit the observed events. This may produce a vague feeling of dissatisfaction with things as they are—from unhappiness with a definite snarl in the progress of events or from mere curiosity. In any event, this is when the problem should be stated in as precise a manner as possible.

Frequently the teacher formulates a realistic problem from the unit concept which he has previously identified. As cited earlier, a concept in the area of science was: Young plants will be almost like their parent plants. From this basic idea the teacher may formulate the problem: How might you identify a plant that has just started growing? He then decides upon an instructional method or technique which seems most appropriate for guiding pupils in solving the problem.

In many instances pupils will be encouraged to develop their own problems, many times for study and analysis. They may arise naturally from various class activities or they may be planned with the help of the teacher. (See Chapter 12, Teacher-Pupil Planning Techniques.)

Analysis of the Problem

The terms of a problem must be clarified, cause and effect relationships must be examined, and the importance of the issue must be established. This involves identifying and evaluating all the important facts and relationships which bear upon the problem.

Establishing Hypotheses

After the pertinent data have been introduced and evaluated, hypotheses for problem solution are offered. These are bold guesses or hunches with respect to the problem. Pupils usually examine those which have been proposed (or even tried) by individuals or groups. They also are encouraged to offer their own suggestions for resolving the difficulty. This is the creative aspect of instruction. Hasty closure on one of the first hypotheses offered should be discouraged.

Reaching a Decision

Although the processes of reflection ultimately result in a decision, the complexity of many instructional problems may render an immediate decision impossible. (See Chapter 9, Discussion Methods.) In any event, however, the learner is encouraged to evolve pertinent generalizations (concepts) from the experience. These will not be identical to the major concept which gave rise to the problem. Rather, they will be supporting concepts which collectively encompass the major concept.

Lesson generalizations are derived by pupils. They are made most meaningful when written out and illustrated. Provision also must be made for their application to new situations, with emphasis on exploration of relationships, comparisons, and prediction of consequences.

VALUES

Emphasis upon concept learning enhances transfer to related areas. Often referred to as *nonspecific transfer*, general ideas (concepts) transfer widely. The "higher" level concepts transfer more readily than do "lower" level concepts.

Concepts provide a basic structure for organizational unit, teaching unit, and lesson planning. Essentially, it is the conceptual framework of an organizational unit which gives order to related experiences.

In terms of basic concepts, evaluation encourages retention of learning.

Concepts tell the learner what *facts* to look for and the meaning to assign to these facts. They are easily stored and rearranged for the derivation of new concepts.

LIMITATIONS AND PROBLEMS

Inadequate concept formation provides a basis for distortions, biases, and prejudices. Since firmly established meanings are accompanied with *feelings*, improper concepts often are difficult to dislodge.

A teacher cannot "give" a pupil a concept. Since meaning is based upon concrete experiences, direct pupil involvement is desirable. Sometimes a mental image (concept) is so clear to the teacher that he is tempted to short-cut the essential learning processes. This temptation is especially great when one is running short of time.

The different levels of concept formation necessitate selection of the appropriate level(s) of learning experiences. Elementary pupils differ widely. Accordingly, group instruction may be ineffective for some of the lesser-prepared pupils.

Teachers who emphasize lesson "topics" tend to attempt too much in a given lesson. Concept formation cannot be crowded or pushed.

It is extremely difficult to determine degree of concept attainment. Since concepts gain meaning through experience, the teacher can never be certain of the optimum number of experiences essential to adequate transfer of learning.

CONCEPT ILLUSTRATIONS

It will be recalled that instructional concepts exist at three different levels: organizational unit (teaching unit themes), teaching unit, and lesson concepts. Lesson concepts (generalizations) are derived *by pupils* as a culminating lesson experience. Essentially they embody one basic teaching unit concept (formulated by the teacher in preplanning activities). Teaching unit concepts, in turn, embody one organizational unit concept. Organizational unit and teaching unit concepts are illustrated below. Lesson generalizations are illustrated in the various chapters dealing with different instructional methods.

Organizational Unit Concepts

I. Useful in the science area (primary grades)
   A. Plants

    B. Animals

    C. Birds

II. Useful in the arithmetic area (kindergarten or first grade)

    A. Personal arithmetic

    B. Money

    C. Counting

    D. Quantity

III. Useful in the language arts area (fourth or fifth grade)

    A. Oral language discussion

    B. Use of the telephone

    C. Story telling

    D. Interviewing procedures

    E. Oral reports

    F. Giving directions

IV. Useful in the social studies area (fifth or sixth grade)

    A. Canada, our northern neighbor

    B. Mexico, our southern neighbor

    C. Our neighbors in Central America

    D. Our neighbors in South America

Teaching Unit Concepts

I. Useful in the science area (primary grades)

Unit: Birds

Concepts:

    A. Birds are helpful because they eat harmful insects.

    B. The birds destroy the seeds of weeds.

    C. Some birds may be kept in the home as pets.

    D. Some birds are beautiful to see.

    E. Some birds make delightful sounds.

II. Useful in the arithmetic area (kindergarten or first grade)

Unit: Personal Arithmetic

Concepts:

    A. Your age is a number.

    B. Your family is a group or set.

    C. Your house number is a location.

    D. Your telephone number is for your safety.

III. Useful in the oral language arts area (fourth or fifth grade)

Unit: Use of the Telephone

Concepts:

    A.   Dialing correctly will get the desired party.

    B.   Securing special services on the telephone, such as the Police Department, Fire Department or Medical Doctor in emergency cases, may save someone's life.

    C.   Telephone standards of speaking will help in communicating with others.

    D.   Respecting the rights of others when using the telephone is a matter of courtesy.

    E.   Using a telephone directory saves time.

IV. Useful in the social studies area (fifth or sixth grade)

Unit: Canada, Our Northern Neighbor

Concepts:

    A.   Physical features of the country affect:

        1. Weather

        2. Vegetation

        3. Areas of population

        4. Industry

    B.   The people of Canada and the United States have many things in common.

    C.   We are dependent upon the land of Canada for many natural resources.

2

ESTABLISHING
INSTRUCTIONAL OBJECTIVES

The most fundamental aspect of teaching is the formulation of worthwhile aims or goals. Just as a list of educational purposes is useful in determining the nature of the curriculum, so do organizational and unit goals guide the teacher and pupil in selection, in organization and, finally, in evaluation of learning experiences. Actually, goals or purposes constitute the hub around which all other instructional activities revolve.

Unless goals are stated in meaningful terms, they do not serve a worthwhile purpose. Although most teachers acknowledge the importance of instructional goals, relatively few use them effectively as a guide for selecting appropriate learning activities. The almost inevitable consequence is an unimaginative, memory-type of experience, commonly known as textbook teaching. When this situation exists, there is a tendency to emphasize textbook facts as ends in themselves. Accordingly, relatively little transfer or application to related life problems can be expected.

Once the teacher has identified major unit concepts to be emphasized, he is in a position to develop unit objectives. Each major concept must be analyzed for the purpose of determining the precise nature of the objective (purpose or goal) to be sought. It may be that an understanding or comprehension is desired; sometimes an attitude or value must be developed and/or altered; frequently a mental or motor skill will be emphasized. This basic decision will determine the nature of the unit experiences.

FUNDAMENTAL PROPERTIES

The ends of instruction (goal attainment) become basic ideas (concepts) in one's repertoire of experience. Ideas are internalized, however, in different ways. For example, one idea may represent a mere basic understanding, while another will be accompanied with strong emotion. Still another idea may be associated with some mental or motor dexterity. All three components usually are related in some measure, with each idea or concept. Nevertheless, the instructional experience will vary considerably with the nature of the outcome sought. Attainment of one does not guarantee the attainment of another.

Cognitive Objectives

Cognitive objectives usually are expressed as *understandings*. They vary from simple recall of facts to highly original and creative ways of combining and synthesizing new ideas and materials. A useful taxonomy of cognitive goals has been developed by Bloom and his associates.[1] They describe six cognitive levels.

1. *Knowledge.* This involves the lowest level of learning including recall and memory. At this level the learner is expected to recall specifics with concrete referents. They include terminology and specific facts such as dates, events, persons, and places. Also included is *recall* of basic principles and generalizations.
2. *Comprehension.* This represents the lowest level of understanding. The individual is able to make use of the materials or ideas without relating them to other materials. For example, he is able to paraphrase or even interpret something he has gained from reading or listening. At the highest level of this category the learner may be able to *extend* his thinking beyond the data by making simple inferences. Thus in the area of science he is able to draw conclusions from a simple demonstration or experiment.
3. *Application.* This intellectual skill entails the use of information in specific situations. The information may be in the form of general ideas, concepts, principals or theories which must be remem-

---

[1] Benjamin S. Bloom, ed., *Taxonomy of Educational Objectives, Handbook I: Cognitive Domain* (New York: David McKay Co., Inc., 1956), David R. Krathwohl, "Stating Objectives Appropriately for Program, for Curriculum, and for Instructional Materials Development," *Journal of Teacher Education* 16, no. 1 (March 1965): 83–92.

bered and applied. For example, the child who draws conclusions from a particular experiment at the comprehension level is now able to *apply* the basic principle(s) to *related* experiments or scientific phenomena.

4. *Analysis.* This involves taking apart the information and making relationships. The purpose is to clarify by discovering hidden meaning and basic structure. The pupil is able to read between the lines, to distinguish between fact and opinion, to assess degree of consistency or inconsistency. Thus he is able to distinguish between relevant and extraneous materials or events and is able to detect unstated assumptions.

5. *Synthesis.* At this level the learner is able to reassemble the component parts for new meaning. This recombining process permits the emergence of a new pattern or structure not previously apparent. Thus the learner may develop new or creative ideas from the process. While a certain amount of combining is involved at the lower levels, at this level the process is more complete. He draws upon elements from many sources *in addition to* the particular problem under consideration. A pupil, for instance, may propose a unique plan (to him at least) for testing a hypothesis. Another pupil may make a discovery or generalization which is not evident from the given communication.

6. *Evaluation.* This highest level of cognition involves making judgments on the materials, information or method for specific purposes. This represents the end process of cognition, involving distinct criteria as a basis for such decisions. When conceived in relation to the problem-solving or cognitive process, it involves selecting one of the proposed alternatives over all the rest.

It is seen from Bloom's taxonomy that intellectual or cognitive learnings vary from simple to the complex, from the concrete to the abstract. Attainment of the higher cognitive levels is dependent on satisfactory progress at the lower levels of cognition. Attainment of the lower levels, however, does not assure attainment of the higher levels. Implicit in the taxonomy are the processes of critical or reflective thinking, sometimes merely described as the problem-solving or cognitive process.

Affective Objectives

Along with the attainment of intellectual or cognitive objectives, teachers have emphasized emotional or affective purposes. Such goals often are expressed as interest, attitudes or appreciations. As Krathwohl, Bloom, and Masia point out, ". . . we need to provide a range of emotion from neutrality through mild to strong emotion, probably of a positive, but possibly also of a negative kind."[2] They have developed such a taxonomy. As with the cognitive domain, the affective taxonomy ranges from the simple to the complex. This is described in terms of relative degrees of *internalization*.[3] By internalization they mean a process through which there is first an incomplete and tentative adoption of the desired emotion to a more complete adoption of the feeling in the latter stages of learning. The five levels of the affective domain follow:

1. *Receiving (Attending).* At this first level the learner merely becomes aware of an idea, process or thing. Thus he is willing to listen or to attend to a given communication. From a purely passive role of captive receiver he may advance to one of directing his attention to the communication, despite competing or distracting stimuli. For example, he listens for rhythm in poetry or prose read aloud.
2. *Responding.* This level involves doing something with or about the phenomenon other than merely perceiving it. At this low level of commitment the pupil does not yet hold the value. To use a common expression of teachers, "He displays an *interest* in the phenomenon." From obedient participation, the pupil may advance to voluntary response, and finally to a *pleasurable feeling* or *satisfaction* which accompanies his behavior. This feeling may be expressed by the goal, "reads poetry for personal pleasure."
3. *Valuing.* As the term implies, at this level a thing, phenomenon or behavior has worth. Behavior at this level reflects a belief or an attitude. Thus it might be said that he "holds the value." This level is characterized by motivated behavior in which the individual's commitment guides his behavior. At the lower end of the continuum the learner might be said to hold the belief somewhat tentatively; at the other end, his value becomes one of conviction—certainty "beyond the shadow of a doubt." Indeed at the upper end of the continuum he is likely to try to persuade others to his way of thinking.

[2] David R. Krathwohl, Benjamin S. Bloom, and Bertram S. Masia, *Taxonomy of Educational Objectives, Handbook II: Affective Domain* (New York: David McKay Co., Inc., 1964), p. 26.

[3] Krathwohl, "Stating Objectives Appropriately," pp. 83–92.

4. *Organization.* Here the individual has established a conscious basis for choice-making. He has organized his values into a system—a set of criteria—for guiding his behavior. Accordingly, he will be able to defend his choices and will be aware of the basis of his attitudes.

5. *Characterization.* At this level the internalizing process is complete. Values are *integrated* into some kind of internally consistent system. Thus the person is described as having certain controlling tendencies. He has a recognized philosophy of life.

Prior to development of the affective taxonomy, teachers experienced considerable difficulty in providing adequate evaluational experiences in this area. Consequently, instructional emphasis tended to neglect the emotional aspects of learning. The affective taxonomy is an extremely useful technique of clarifying the problem.

Complex affective goals are not as easily achieved as complex cognitive goals. Indeed the levels of "organization" and "characterization" are not reached in any one school year. They represent a culmination of many years of educational experience.

Psychomotor Objectives

A third major instructional domain is in the area of mental and motor skills. As a result of certain instructional activities, teachers recognize that pupils should acquire such motor skills as cutting with scissors or playing ball, and also that they should develop certain mental skills such as those required in writing and talking. Although all skills require some understanding and are usually accompanied with varying degrees of emotion, it is recognized that *emphasis* in this area must be placed upon development of the skill. The psychomotor taxonomy clarifies the essentials of this process.

1. *Observing.* At this level the learner observes a more experienced person in his performance of the activity. Usually he is asked to observe sequences and relationships and to pay particular attention to the finished product. Sometimes the reading of directions substitutes for this experience. Frequently, however, reading is *supplemented* by direct observation. Thus the beginning ball player may read his manual and then watch his teacher demonstrate certain techniques.

2. *Imitating.* By the time the learner has advanced to this level he has begun to acquire the basic rudiments of the desired behavior. He follows directions and sequences under close supervision. The total act is not important, nor is timing or coordination emphasized. He is conscious of a deliberate effort to imitate the model. The ball player, for example, may practice a prescribed way of fielding the ball.

3. *Practicing.* The entire sequence is performed repeatedly at this level. All aspects of the act are performed in sequence. Conscious effort is no longer necessary as the performance becomes more or less habitual in nature. At this level we might reasonably say that the person has acquired the skill.

4. *Adapting.* The terminal level is often referred to as "perfection of the skill." Although a few individuals develop much greater skill in certain areas than do most individuals, there is nearly always room for "greater perfection." The process involves adapting "minor" details which, in turn, influence the total performance. Such modifications may be initiated by the learner or by his teacher. This is the process a ball player goes through, for example, when a good player becomes a better player.

It is obvious that the psychomotor domain also involves a graded sequence from simple to complex. By deciding upon the degree of skill development needed, the teacher is able to plan his instructional activities most efficiently. Likewise, evaluational techniques will vary considerably with the different levels.

GOAL FORMULATION

For many years teachers have been stating worthwhile goals. Unfortunately, however, goals have been stated so vaguely as to hold little real meaning. The result has been overemphasis on textbook teaching and relatively little application to related life problems. The procedure recommended below represents one way of correcting the difficulty.

Writing Goals

When achieved, an instructional goal is internalized as an idea or concept. However, the nature of ideas will vary, according to the three broad domains previously described. Either stated or implied in a worthy goal is a real-life application. As a means of focusing attention upon the pupil, it is recommended that each instructional goal begin with the introductory clause, "After this unit (or lesson) the pupil should. . . ." In this way the emphasis tends to be shifted from teacher wants to pupil needs.

The next step is identification of the domain to be emphasized. The words *understanding, attitudes and appreciations,* and *skills and habits* are commonly employed to denote the cognitive, affective, and psychomotor domains respectively. For example, "After this lesson the pupil should have furthered his *understanding* of. . . ." Each goal should be restricted to a given domain and to a single idea.

Identifying Behavioral Outcomes

Although learnings are internalized as ideas or concepts, there are many outward manifestations of that which is learned. A pupil's behavior offers the best clues to that which is learned. These are referred to as behavioral outcomes. For each instructional goal a number of pupil outcomes will suggest goal achievement or means to achievement. Accordingly, for each goal the teacher should select those specific behavioral outcomes which seem most likely to reflect progress toward goal achievement. It is usually desirable to identify as many outcomes as possible and then to select those which seem most practical for use as a guide to instructional activities.

Often behavioral outcomes are incorporated within the goal framework. For example, after reading the story about an immigrant family, the pupil should further appreciate the social inequalities as evidenced by the following: (1) His realistic *responses* in a class discussion on the problem "What should be the United State's policy with respect to immigrant people?" (2) His willingness to examine feeling reactions resulting from a dramatic play designed to portray feelings in a specified social situation. (3) His greater cooperation in school with children who dress differently or speak with an accent. It should be noted that outcomes (2) and (3) suggest different levels of number three (valuing) of this domain. By becoming thoroughly familiar with the various levels of each instructional domain, the teacher can select those outcomes which seem most appropriate for any given set of circumstances.

Unit outcomes provide definite clues to desirable class activities. The foregoing illustration, for example, pinpoints at least two *intermediate* behaviors which might be elicited as avenues to goal achievement. This applies to outcomes (1) and (2). Outcome (3) is a terminal behavior but one which can hardly be measured under normal school conditions. Its usefulness seems to be primarily that of reminding the teacher of the ultimate behavior being sought.

In *evaluating goal achievement*, the teacher must direct attention to *terminal* behaviors. The behaviors identified in the foregoing illustration, however, provide a useful *basis* for this task. Outcome (1), for example, can be rendered sufficient for evaluational purposes by identifying various processes essential in a problem-solving class discussion. These might include one's ability (1) to identify the central issue, (2) to recognize assumptions, (3) to evaluate evidence, and (4) to draw warranted conclusions.

VALUES

The appropriate formulation of goals provides the basis for the development of consistent learning and evaluation experiences.

The process of formulating goals, in terms of behavioral outcomes, emphasizes the transfer of learnings to related areas.

The preliminary formulation of lesson goals, with their appropriate behavioral outcomes, tends to expand one's perception of the many avenues available for reaching these ends. Thus a variety of instructional techniques may be employed.

The appropriate goal formulation tends to relegate the selected textbook to its proper place, as only one of many instructional resources.

LIMITATIONS AND PROBLEMS

Goals or aims, when inappropriately formulated, are a waste of time. Thus many teachers consider them the *least* important rather than the *most* important aspect of the instructional process.

Many worthy instructional outcomes cannot be observed or evaluated within the context of a given classroom. As a consequence, certain important learning experiences may be minimized, simply because they cannot be evaluated effectively. One solution to the problem involves the formulation of longitudinal goals, evaluated by several teachers over an extended period of time.

Since each pupil is expected to progress toward common goal achievement, there is a tendency for some teachers to follow with a common set of learning and evaluational activities. Such a practice ignores all that we know about individual differences. Different pupils achieve instructional outcomes in different ways.

Many worthwhile goals can be derived for each instructional unit. There is a tendency to emphasize the cognitive over the affective domain. Again, this practice apparently is related to the ease of evaluating cognitive, as opposed to affective, learning. With the recent appearance of a taxonomy of educational objectives in the affective domain, it is hoped that this imbalance will be adjusted.

Considerable confusion exists between those behaviors sought *during* the learning experience and those sought as *terminal* behaviors. The teacher's first concern must be with those behaviors which are likely to contribute to growth toward goals. Eventually, however, he must direct attention toward final goal achievement. The latter must be more specific than the former.

ILLUSTRATIONS

Additional unit goal illustrations are provided in Appendixes A, B, and C. Lesson goals are illustrated in the sample lesson plans provided in each methods chapter.

3

PLANNING FOR TEACHING

Planning, like map making, enables one to predict the future course of events. In essence, a plan is a blueprint—a plan of action. As any traveler knows, the best-laid plans can go awry. Sometimes unforeseen circumstances even prevent one from beginning a well-planned journey; other times, conditions while on the trip may cause one to alter his plans drastically. More often, however, a well-planned journey is altered in *minor* ways for those unpredictable "side trips" which may seem desirable from close range.

Likewise, teachers must plan classroom experiences. They must plan the scope and sequence for learning activities, the subject matter to be utilized, the units to be taught, and the tests to be given. While few teachers would deny the necessity of planning, there is some controversy with respect to the scope and nature of planning. Indeed, methods specialists themselves differ relative to the essential scope of planning. Some seem to feel that unit planning renders lesson planning almost unnecessary. Others stress the importance of lesson plans while minimizing the value of unit plans. While the planning needs of teachers will vary markedly, there is considerable justification for *both* unit and lesson planning.

THE ORGANIZATIONAL UNIT

An over-all organizational unit perspective is achieved by listing major ideas, problems, and topics which seem appropriate for the area of study. The most obvious aids in developing an organizational unit are the selected textbooks and resource materials available. Also needed is a collection of other textbooks, library books, and study aids in the curriculum area. Although organizational units often are prepared by each individual teacher, increased emphasis is being given to joint participation of teachers in the same grade level within the school. This enables teachers to develop desirable commonalities. At the same time, it leaves the individual teacher free to develop each teaching unit in his own way.

The organizational unit involves a series of steps leading up to planning a teaching unit. It provides an essential foundation for a subsequent teaching unit and lesson plan. Careless planning at this level endangers the entire educational experience.

Organizational Unit Concepts

After inspecting various resources in the area, the teacher formulates a few basic organizational unit concepts. They will be very broad and suggestive only. There may be as many as a dozen of these. To illustrate from an organizational unit in the area of art for upper grades:

1. Art is a means of communication.
2. Art has cultural and aesthetic values.
3. Art helps children learn arithmetic, science, reading or any other curriculum area.

After several tentative organizational unit concepts have been stated, they are revised and reworked until four to eight basic ideas remain. (Some teachers prefer to incorporate these concepts into teaching objectives. This step is not essential, however.)

Organizational Unit and Major Teaching Units

Major teaching units are developed from the organizational unit concepts described above. Teaching unit titles will reflect basic themes implicit in the major concepts. Frequently a need for two or more teaching units may be developed from a single major concept. This suggests the need for more specific concepts. Eventually there will be a teaching unit for each major concept. Appropriate teaching unit titles, based upon the illustrated concepts in an area of art, follow:

1. Art communicates.
2. Art values.
3. Art enhances learning.

After major teaching units have been tentatively established, an approximate time schedule is established to reflect relative degrees of emphasis to be given to each unit. It may be that time limitations will necessitate basic changes. Sometimes certain proposed teaching units must be deleted. Teaching units are seldom less than two or more than four weeks long; however, the interest and maturity of the pupils will determine the length of the teaching unit.

Organizational Unit Introduction

After major teaching units have been selected, the teacher can develop for pupils an overview of the major aspects for the school year. The purpose of this experience is to give students an opportunity to develop a series of expectations relative to the curriculum area. Basic purposes, at their level of understanding, are offered. Pupils, in turn, are provided an opportunity to ask questions and to offer suggestions. The effect of such an experience is to create initial interest in the experiences which are to follow.

THE TEACHING UNIT

Unit planning is designed to center the work of the school around meaningful wholes or patterns and to make the work of different days focus on a central theme until some degree of unified learning is attained. The process is one of combining related ideas into some intellectual pattern. It provides opportunities for critical thinking, generalization, and application of ideas to many situations. As indicated in the previous discussion, unit themes do *not* correspond to textbook units. The unit concept approaches what Jerome Bruner has termed the basic structure of knowledge.[1]

Implicit in unit planning are three different phases: initiating activities, developing activities, and culminating activities. The first phase of unit planning is similar to the steps in planning an organizational unit. Unit planning is necessarily more restricted and specific than the latter. In all cases, however, the process must be consistent with, and fit into, the over-all framework established in the organizational unit.

Unit Concepts

From the particular organizational unit concept, a number of teaching unit concepts will be developed. Each of these must contribute to development of the over-all unit theme. The teaching unit length will reflect the number and complexity of teaching unit concepts to be developed. To illustrate from organizational unit concept 1, cited on page 20, "Art is a means of communication," the following unit concepts can be developed:

1. Art creates interest.
2. Art presents facts.
3. Art facilitates comparisons.
4. Art expresses relationships.
5. Art presents concepts pictorially.

Teaching Unit Goals

Based upon teaching unit concepts, appropriate unit goals and their accompanying outcomes are developed. Unit goals provide a necessary transition from what the teacher views as the ends of instruction to statements of pupil behaviors necessary for and indicative of the desired learnings. Frequently each unit goal will embody a different unit concept, but sometimes two or more *may* be embodied within a single goal. Indeed there are usually more concepts than goals. To illustrate from the five concepts cited above:

[1] Jerome Bruner, *The Process of Education* (Cambridge, Mass.: Harvard University Press, 1961), pp. 17–18.

1. After this unit the pupil should have furthered his understanding that art presents facts, as evidenced by the following:
   a. His ability to apply appropriate facts in a drawing that he makes.
   b. His interpretation of the facts presented in a drawing by a written explanation.
2. After this unit the pupil should have furthered his understanding of how art expresses relationships and facilitates comparisons by the following:
   a. His ability to interpret art drawings showing relationships and comparisons in a class discussion.
   b. His ability to apply appropriate relationships and comparisons in a single drawing test.

Goal 1 apparently relates to concept 2, cited on page 22, while Goal 2 relates to both concepts 3 and 4 cited on page 22. The behavioral outcomes suggest specific methods and techniques which seem appropriate *means* of goal achievement.[2]

Teaching Unit Introduction (Initiating Phase)

It seems desirable to assist pupils in gaining an over-all perspective of the unit by suggesting purposes and activities to be pursued during the unit. It is designed to create a state of readiness for things to come. This is the initiating phase of the unit.

Subject Matter

As an aid in developing a series of cohesive experiences a subject-matter outline should be developed. Various activities of the unit rest upon this outline. Some teachers prefer detailed outlines; others favor topical outlines. The latter is illustrated in the sample teaching units provided in the Appendixes.

Learning Experiences (Developing Phase)

If teaching unit outcomes are stated in specific terms, most of the learning experiences will be identified there. Nevertheless, it is

[2] Unit goals are more fully treated in the previous chapter.

desirable to list all major activities in one place to facilitate adequate preparation for these experiences. This also enables the teacher to develop a desirable sequence of activities and to establish certain priorities. For example:

1. Class Discussion.
   Problem: What can we do to communicate to the Russian people details of our way of life?
2. Letter Writing.
   Problem: What information can you provide about the U.S.S.R.?
3. Oral Reporting.
   Problem: What articles and pictures portray the Russian people and culture?
4. Construction Activity.
   Problem: Which country has the largest land mass, the United States or Russia?[3]

The act of preplanning some of the activities does not mean that the teacher must assume the role of taskmaster. Pupils may participate actively in the planning of class activities, but this does not replace the need for a certain number of preplanned activities *suggested* by the teacher. As in the sample unit, different pupils often will be involved in different activities; thus provision for individual differences may become a reality. For beginning teachers it may be necessary to make a special point of this in the unit plan.

Unit Evaluation (Culminating Phase)

A unit plan is incomplete without some forecast of progress toward the teaching unit goals. Teaching unit plans may be rendered ineffective if pupils anticipate being asked to recall specific facts only from a textbook. Measurement and evaluation must be consistent with the teaching unit goals and anticipated behavioral outcomes. As indicated in the previous chapter, behaviors which are appropriate as learning activities usually are not adequate for evaluating learning. They do provide sound bases, however, for development of the needed evaluational experiences. For example, the letter writing activity (cited in the foregoing illustrations

---

[3] For a more complete list of activities see the Appendixes.

of learning activities) should help pupils learn the proper form for letter writing. Thus test items based on another letter might well be utilized to evaluate their knowledge of the proper form for letter writing.

LESSON PLANNING

A lesson plan is an expanded portion of a teaching unit plan. It represents a detailed analysis of a particular *activity* described in the teaching unit plan. For example, one of the teaching unit outcomes anticipated in the sample teaching unit was the pupil's "ability to relate the revolt in Russia to the Communist Party." This led to the provision for an *activity* called *learning analysis report*. While the activity was stated in the teaching unit plan, no indication was given as to *how* the activity would be developed. In developing pupil activities, careful planning is essential. The lesson plan serves such a purpose.

The essentials of a lesson plan are somewhat similar to the important elements of a teaching unit plan. Although forms and styles differ markedly from one teacher to another, a lesson plan usually contains a goal, lesson introduction (approach), lesson development, and lesson summary. Depending on the nature of the lesson, it also may include a list of materials needed, provision for individual differences, and an assignment.

The common elements of lesson planning erroneously suggest a standard routine. While it is true that most plans will be structured around the common elements described, significant differences will be observed within this framework. Different teaching methods often are designed for different instructional purposes; they involve different sequences. Thus lesson plans must be modified accordingly. Sample lesson plans, prepared for the purposes of illustrating each of the major teaching methods, appear in the respective methods chapters. A comparison of some of these plans is recommended. The particular style of lesson planning illustrated in this book is suggestive only.

Teaching Unit Concept

Each lesson plan is based upon a teaching *unit* outcome, deemed essential for achievement of a teaching *unit* concept. Thus behind every lesson plan is a concept. Two or more lessons may be essential to

insure the attainment of a single concept. It is desirable to restate the concept prior to development of a lesson plan. Although Woodruff[4] has suggested that in certain contexts the concept may be stated for pupil guidance, most authorities feel that pupils should be guided inductively toward concept achievement.[5]

Lesson Goals

From each teaching unit concept the teacher must decide what major goal domain must be emphasized, e.g., cognitive, affective or psychomotor. It may be that two or even all three of these should receive emphasis. Usually there will be a different lesson for each major goal domain to be emphasized. Sometimes, however, more than one domain may be stressed in a single lesson. This applies especially to the method of teacher-pupil planning which involves several unified lessons.

By way of illustration, teaching unit concept 4 is reproduced along with unit goal 2.

Teaching Unit Concept: Art expresses relationships.
Teaching Unit Goal: After this unit the pupil should have furthered his understanding of how art expresses relationships and comparisons, as evidenced by the following:

1. His ability to interpret art drawings showing relationships and comparisons in a class discussion.
2. His ability to apply appropriate relationships and comparisons in a simple drawing test.

Unit outcome 1 suggests class discussion and the cognitive domain (although the affective domain can be stressed in certain types of discussion). Thus using the teaching unit concept as a guide, a lesson goal, with appropriate lesson outcomes, can be derived. For example, after this lesson

---

[4] Aashel D. Woodruff, *Basic Concepts of Teaching* (San Francisco, Calif.: Chandler Publishing Co., 1961).
[5] Kenneth H. Hoover and Paul M. Hollingsworth, *Learning and Teaching in the Elementary School* (Boston: Allyn and Bacon, Inc., 1970), Chapter 3.

the pupil should have furthered his understanding of how art expresses relationships and comparisons, as evidenced by (1) the questions he asks during the discussion, (2) his ability to offer and/or evaluate hypotheses posed during the discussion, and (3) his ability to derive generalizations from the discussion.

It will be noted that the specific learning outcomes represent behaviors which can be expected during a problem-solving discussion experience.

Lesson Goal and Introduction

Once the teacher decides his lesson goal he is in a position to formulate an appropriate discussion problem. To illustrate: What relationships or comparisons do you find in this drawing? Many teachers prefer to place the problem before pupils for the purpose of guiding discussion.

Lesson Development

Major activities of the lesson are incorporated in this phase of a lesson plan. Subdivisions of the lesson development will vary with the particular method to be used. The teacher must first identify the different aspects of the reflective process germane to the particular method involved. He then writes out points, questions, and/or comments deemed essential in the instructional process. In class discussion, for example, this may consist of only two or three key questions in each area to be explored. At this point the reader will want to study the illustrated lesson plans provided in the methods chapters.

Deriving Generalizations and Lesson Summary

The culminating portion of a lesson is often neglected or rushed. This is particularly unfortunate, since it is at this point that pupils are expected to derive concepts or generalizations. The summary of almost every lesson should involve pupils in the derivation of generalizations, based on the current lesson experiences. The lesson generalizations are equal, collectively, to the basic unit (lesson) concept upon which the lesson rests. Thus any one lesson generalization cannot be identical to the basic unit (lesson) concept.

Lesson generalizations should be derived by pupils. Some authorities insist that they be written out by pupils.[6] In many instances pupils will verbally derive lesson generalizations which are written for all to see.

Basic unit (lesson) concepts, then, are derived by teachers as they plan for instruction. At this level, concepts are discussed during review lessons, treated in a subsequent chapter. As an aid in teaching, the classroom teacher usually writes out one or two anticipated concepts in his lesson plan summary. They are to be used as an instructional guide only. To illustrate from the cited lesson problem:

1. Relationships can be illustrated in drawings.
2. Drawings can be used to show comparisons.

VALUES

Unit planning provides a basic subject matter structure around which specific classroom activities can be organized.

Through careful unit planning, the teacher is able to integrate the basic subject matter concepts and those of related areas into meaningful teaching experiences.

Unit planning enables the teacher to provide adequate balance between various dimensions of subject matter. By taking a long-range look he is able to develop essential priorities in advance of actual classroom experiences.

The organizational and teaching unit plans seem to be the best techniques yet developed to enable a teacher to break away from traditional textbook teaching.

Emphasis upon behavioral outcomes in teaching units and lesson plans tends to result in a more meaningful series of learning experiences.

[6] William H. Burton, Roland B. Kimball, and Richard L. Wing, *Education for Effective Thinking* (New York: Appleton-Century-Crofts, Inc., 1960), p. 163.

LIMITATIONS AND PROBLEMS

A teacher may become a "slave" to his plans. This is a special hazard
for those who prefer detailed lesson plans.

Excessive planning may promote an authoritarian class situation. This
factor may become apparent when the changing needs of pupils are
largely disregarded.

Unless adequate caution is exercised, lesson plans may become a mere outline of textbook materials. If practical lesson goals, along with specific
behavioral outcomes, are developed *as a basis for* class activities, this
need not be a hazard.

Thorough planning takes time—more time, in fact, than is available to
some first-year teachers. Furthermore, usually it is impractical to
construct lesson plans more than three or four days in advance of the
experience. (By making substantial use of marginal notes a teacher
may use effective plans as a basis for subsequent planning.)

ILLUSTRATIONS

Unit plans are illustrated in the Appendixes. Lesson plans
are provided in each of the chapters dealing with instructional methods.

4

ORGANIZING FOR INDIVIDUAL DIFFERENCES

In order to meet the educational needs of the individual pupil, the teacher must organize the learning environment for each child in his classroom. One of the basic tenets of education in our democracy is that "every child has a right to a free, public school education *commensurate with his abilities*." For every child to receive an education commensurate with his abilities, the classroom environment must be organized for the individual differences each child possesses. Group productivity and individual achievement are enhanced if the teacher provides learning experiences in which each child can succeed.

FUNDAMENTAL PROPERTIES

In providing for individual differences within the classroom, the teacher must recognize the unique differences among the children and the varying needs of the pupils assigned to him. An effective program must be organized with appropriate instructional patterns and materials to meet these needs and to match the pupil's different responses to the appropriate teaching method or technique.

The Unique Child

Each child is the product of his inherited traits, the environment in which he lives, his reaction to his environment, and the people with whom he comes in contact. The teacher soon learns that the children in his classroom differ from one another in every conceivable way. It is the master teacher who readily admits these differences and goes about the task of assessing the needs of each child and then develops teaching strategies to meet these needs.

A child learns more effectively when he is presented with learning opportunities in the form of materials and tasks for which he is ready. Learning is enhanced when each child is appropriately rewarded for his correct responses and when he meets not only the teacher's expectations for him, but also his expectations for himself.

Instructional Patterns

Organizing for individual differences implies some type of an instructional pattern which will aid pupils in the learning process. Grouping children together for instruction may be one way to approach individual differences among children. Many teachers avoid grouping, while espousing individual instruction; however, the purpose for grouping is to provide for individual differences. If within a group, attention is *not* directed toward individuals within that group, then grouping loses its purpose.

Organizing instruction on an individual basis is a second fundamental instructional pattern for meeting differences among children. The child essentially works by himself without the group. Curriculum materials are made available for his use whereby he paces himself in a self-instructional manner. As described in the previous chapter the unit plan combines both group and individual instruction. Unit planning gives the classroom teacher opportunities to provide for pupil differences within his room. Individual competencies and interests are built within the unit structure and the teacher, through careful planning, is able to involve pupils in activities which are not beyond the child's achievement level.

Instructional Materials

Instructional materials should be selected with the needs of each child well in mind. If the materials are used meaningfully, the selection must be based on the knowledge of each pupil's abilities, his achievement level, and his interests. This means that the teacher must have available to him the results of periodic achievement tests, teacher-made diagnostic tests, and pupil interest inventories.

Meeting the problems of differences requires considerable flexibility by the teacher in the use of instructional materials. Sometimes the teacher may adapt the materials for group use. At other times, specific materials should be available so children may work not only individually, but also at certain periods without the constant supervision and direction of the teacher.

GROUPING

When it becomes necessary for the teacher to initiate grouping within his classroom, there are obvious steps the teacher must follow. Grouping must be based on the knowledge of each child's abilities, his achievement level, and his interest in the various subject matter areas of the curriculum.

The modern approach to grouping is that it should be as flexible as possible. Children should have an opportunity to work in many different groups throughout the school day. A child may work in one reading group and then shift to work with a different group in social studies, and still a different group in science. The elementary schoolteacher may employ at least six different types of grouping in his classroom plans.

Achievement Groups

Children within the classroom may be grouped according to their achievement levels in one or many different areas of curriculum. For instance, a child could be in several ability groups: one for reading, one for arithmetic, and one for science.

The achievement level of the child would be ascertained by achievement tests, standardized tests, learning aptitude tests, informal tests, plus the teacher's observation. These tests would guide the teacher in selecting the various achievement groups. After the children are grouped, the teacher must maintain group flexibility because some children may function better in a different group. Some children may be adjusted to easier or more difficult groups to approximate more nearly their individual functioning levels.

This recommended grouping procedure is made wholly on the basis of achievement rather than on the basis of ability. If the system works properly, the eventual grouping *actually* will approach one based on ability.

Special Need Groups

It may be discovered while working with the children throughout the day that several children from various groups are having difficulty in understanding a specific problem. For example, certain children from several reading groups may be called together to form a "special need group" for learning diphthongs in phonetic analysis.

The special need group will be disbanded when the children learn the specific technique or solve the problem they have in common. This type of grouping could involve children from each achievement group and several special need groups could be organized in the classroom at the same time.

Interest Groups

A third type of grouping within the classroom is the interest group, which is formed among children who share the same or similar interests. Children who are interested in a particular topic such as dinosaurs would share with one another information they have collected from various sources. Class projects, school reports, and construction activities are just a few learning experiences that could be produced in interest groups.

Children who have similar hobbies also could be formed into interest groups. Many hobbies relate very well to various areas of the curriculum and may be an additional source for learning when children are formed into an interest-hobby group.

Team Groups

In team grouping, two children work together as a team concerning a particular problem which is common to both. For example, in the reading area, two children who make omission errors in oral reading could be teamed together. One child could read orally while the second child would circle the omission errors the reader made thus helping each child become aware of his inaccurate oral reading problem.

Research Groups

This type of grouping may be used with two or more children. The group task is to research a particular topic. Research groups could be formed for panel discussions as explained in Chapter 9, construction activities or classroom reports.

Full Class Group

There are many times when the entire class should work together as a single unit. Learning activities that are common for all pupils in the classroom could be introduced to the entire class at one time. For example, activities such as listening lessons, choral reading, dramatizations, reporting, class and panel discussion are appropriate for the full class group.

INDIVIDUALIZING

Procedures to provide for individual differences in the classroom may be seen in many different forms throughout this country. The concept of *individualized instruction*, which involves a wide range of efforts to tailor the educational program of the schools to the individual learner, has brought about new administrative arrangements and instructional programs.

Each of these programs has been tried with enthusiasm at one time or another as a possible solution to the problem of individualizing instruction. Many of these programs have *individualized* instruction, but many do not have *personalized* instruction—that is, no one arrangement or program has yet completely succeeded in meeting *all* the individual needs of the diversity of children in the public schools. Even though *all* the individual needs may not be met by these approaches, some of these innovations may be utilized in the classroom by the teacher.

Pupil Tutors

Through this approach, individualizing instruction is accomplished by using pupil tutors. This program should *not* be simply a matter of allowing advanced sixth grade children to tutor first and second grade children who have experienced some difficulty in learning a specific skill. Pupil tutors should be taught the processes and skills involved in tutoring before they begin.

After the pupil tutors understand their duties, children from upper grades may assist children needing special tutors in the lower grades. This cross-grade tutoring not only aids the child being tutored but also is beneficial to the tutor as he gains more insight in the particular skill taught. Children within the same classroom also may be used as tutors for their fellow classmates.

Continuous Progress Plan

This plan is to provide for the uninterrupted growth in learning of each child without restrictions as to specific materials or modes of instruction. Teachers are encouraged to individually adapt this plan within their own classrooms. The goal of the continuous progress plan is that each child will receive appropriate learning experiences for his individual needs.

In this plan, grade level restrictions are not considered important as long as the teacher and pupil work purposefully from one sequential learning activity to the next.[1] Under the concept of continuous progress, a child does not fail a grade. Each child merely begins work in the new school year where he stopped at the close of the preceding year.

Learning Packages

Learning Activity Packages, Contracts, UNIPACS, Performance Criteria Units, Teaching-Learning Units, and many other names are used to identify learning packages. Whatever the name it might have, the learning packages are instructional modules that contain one or more instructional objectives most often stated in behavioral terms. Usually the

---

[1] In effect, then, the teacher will time and pace the child in accordance with what he knows about the *learning process*, the *learner*, and the *materials* to be learned.

packages contain a pre-test, sample test items or other criteria which suggest how the behavior will be measured, a bibliography of study references, and a list of instructional materials that are available to help the pupil accomplish the behavioral objectives.

These learning packages are designed to free both the teacher and the pupils from group instruction. The children pace themselves through the learning packages. During the time that a child completes one learning package, another child may complete several packages; thus, no child must pace his rate of learning to a group standard.

Many teachers make learning packages to fit their particular requirements for the children in their classrooms. However, commercially developed and tested learning packages are available for teachers and schools who do not have the time or resources to produce their own.

Individually Prescribed Instruction

A goal of individually prescribed instruction is to provide a variety of instructional materials and techniques to meet the individual needs of pupils. The individually prescribed instructional materials are carefully sequenced and empirically developed according to detailed behavioral objectives.

In this program, each child has a thorough diagnosis or diagnostic pre-test to determine what the child has mastered in a specific curriculum area and what he has yet to learn. The pupils are then expected to proceed through prepared materials relevant to instructional objectives as determined by the pre-tests. Ideally, pupils are expected to work at their own rates rather than to work with the whole class. No child need slow down his learning to accomodate the rate of a group of other children. The pupil who is a fast learner may move as rapidly as his development dictates. The opposite is also true—the slow learner is not pushed beyond his learning intake.

Once the placement testing is completed, the teacher determines the starting point for each child. On the basis of this diagnosis of a pupil's weaknesses, a prescription is developed for each child. This prescription lists the materials in which he should begin his study.

The pupil generally begins work independently on the prescribed materials. Most of the pupils can proceed through these materials with a minimum amount of teacher direction and instruction. As the child is working independently, the teacher is free for instructional decision-making, tutoring, evaluation of pupil progress, and the scoring of worksheets and tests.

After the pupil finishes work on the prescribed materials, post-instructional tests are administered to determine how well he has mastered them. These tests are also used to prescribe the next instructional unit.

LEARNING CENTER

The importance of developing learner self-direction in individualizing instruction has long been recognized. For individualizing instruction and development of independent work habits, school libraries have been an accepted part of the educational scene. What is new is the emphasis on the library as a central part of the educational experience and its expansion to include many types of instructional materials in addition to books. The term *learning center*, or *instructional resource center*, more nearly describes the facility provided in today's schools where films, tapes, filmstrips, programmed materials, recordings, models, and other non-book materials are incorporated into one collection along with the more traditional printed materials. Some schools have organized the learning center as a separate part from the library. However it is organized, the learning resource center has become a learning laboratory, rather than a museum or quiet retreat.

Learning Center Needs

The learning center in the modern elementary school is not the concern of the librarian or audiovisual teacher alone; it is central to the work of all teachers. Therefore every teacher should have a broad general concept of what is needed to meet the demands of independent study.

A *varied and extensive collection of materials* related to curriculum needs and the personal needs and interests of young people is the first consideration. All types of materials should be available, and they should be organized in such a way that pupils can readily find what is needed.

The needs of the slower learner and the poor reader, as well as those of the superior pupil, must be kept in mind. Materials should be selected by teachers and learning center personnel working together, and the budget should be sufficient to allow for replacement of worn and obsolete materials as well as the acquisition of new materials to meet new demands. Duplication of much-used materials is necessary to provide for large numbers of pupils.

The rapid growth of educational technology is revolutionizing the school learning center. The larger machines for classroom use of films, filmstrips, records, and transparencies are being supplemented by smaller and less expensive models which permit pupils to use these materials *as individuals*. Copying machines are now available in many learning centers to eliminate the tedious copying of materials by hand from noncirculating reference works. Teaching machines of all types are appearing in learning centers. The pupil carrel of the future probably will be an elaborate console at which the pupil may hear recordings and tapes, view films and filmstrips, use video tapes, and record his responses.

The learning resource center should include sufficient convenient storage space for the present materials collection with room for expansion. Work areas are needed for book processing and for the production of audio-visual materials, and work spaces should be provided for large numbers of pupils and teachers. These spaces should be divided to allow for private individual work, including listening and viewing by the individual, and somewhat larger and more elaborately equipped spaces for small group work. Newer schools are providing private study areas, or carrels, for from 25 to 40 percent of their enrollment.

The program of services and instruction includes much more than the checking out of books and other materials. Skilled reference help must be available at all times, and this should include assistance in using non-book materials as well as in locating material in print. Professional staff members should have time for conferences with teachers; also staff members should be available for classroom visits or instruction of groups of pupils within the resource learning center. There must be a constant flow of materials from the center to the classroom.

Pupil use of the learning center is the final measure of its success. Not only should the pupil be welcome there, he must have *time* to go there. Pupil schedules must allow time for independent study within the school day, and the rules governing his movement in and out of the learning center must be as simple and nonrestrictive as possible.

Learning Center Reinforces the Classroom

Many teachers do not realize fully the potential of the learning center and the instructional materials collection for the improvement of their classroom performance—they are content to depend almost entirely upon textbooks. Yet supplementary materials can provide much more information for the pupil than can possibly be presented in the best textbook and, often, in a much more interesting way. Where the text merely summarizes and generalizes, supplementary material particularizes, makes vivid and specific, and adds color and interest to what the text can outline.

The individualization of instruction, now recognized to be the greatest need in education, must be based on a wide variety of available material if it is to be more than a popular catchword. Not only must there be materials for the investigation of many facets of a given subject, but the materials collection must provide the same information at widely varying degrees of difficulty. There must be something to challenge the brightest student as well as give satisfaction to the dullest and slowest. The needs of a class one year may be quite different from those of a new class the following year. Textbooks and small classroom collections cannot provide for individualization; use of the central materials collection is essential.

Skill in independent study can be attained only through practice, on assignments of increasing complexity. As the pupil's success in this area increases, so does his ability to learn independently and his willingness to assume some responsibility for his own learning. Providing the needed experience in this area is a joint responsibility of the teacher and the learning center specialist.

INTEREST CENTERS

In addition to learning centers, which are essentially a total school operation, interest centers in each individual classroom are needed to assist the pupils in the development of independent work habits. Just as a classroom library is supplemental to a school library, so the interest centers are supplemental to a learning center. The term *interest center*, or *learning station*, more nearly describes areas of the room in which the teacher or pupils have established a place in which interests are developed and problems may be more fully explored.

Centers of Interest

Depending upon the interests and the maturity of the pupils in the classroom, many different interest centers may be established. Centers of interest could be the reading center, library corner, play corner, science center, arithmetic center, painting center, sharing center, music center, listening station, and the like.

Interest Center Needs

Elaborate materials and space are *not* needed to develop interest centers in the classroom. A table, some chairs, and bookcases will make an interesting center. A bulletin board will also add to the center if one is available. Cardboard or wooden packing boxes can be remodeled and turned into tables or bookcases when tables, chairs, and bookcases are not available. One side of a cardboard box covered with cloth can make a bulletin board.

Children can make or bring to the center various materials, books, magazines, specimens and exhibits, magnets, aquariums, games, puzzles, etc., which could be shared and add interest in the classroom. For a listening center a record player, tape or cassette recorder and headphones should be supplied with tapes, records, or cassette tapes.

Interest Centers Reinforce Instruction and Learning

The interest center or learning station reinforces classroom experiences and learning. The centers also develop and extend pupil interests as well as enrich the lives of the pupils in the classroom. Individualization of instruction as well as independent work habits can also be developed through interest centers and learning stations.

VALUES

Grouping increases the potential for *individualizing* instruction.
Through grouping or individualizing instruction, each pupil has an opportunity to meet the goals of instruction, commensurate with his capacities.

Competition with one's own progress is possible through individualization of instruction.

A variety of grouping and individualizing techniques are available for the teacher because no one technique for adapting instruction to pupil differences may be considered superior to others. Rather, a combination of techniques is desirable.

Individual instruction allows the child to pace himself in the learning process; he need not be held to the achievement progress of other children.

Grouping instruction provides for the children's social and emotional needs.

LIMITATIONS AND PROBLEMS

Grouping within the classroom *should not* be done just for the sake of grouping, rather, its purpose is to direct *attention to individuals* within the group.

Sub-grouping within a given class must be flexible; however, many teachers do not shift children from one group to another when the need arises.

Class groups must be handled so as to minimize any feelings of stigma or superiority associated with different groupings.

Giving identical assignments to all pupils in a given group is little better than no grouping at all.

Careful advance planning is essential for organizing for individual differences. The teacher who is not able or willing to do careful planning should not embark on such a method of teaching.

ILLUSTRATED GROUPING PROCEDURES

Organizing for Individual Differences

Initial instruction may be made to a group or the entire class by the teacher or pupil. The children individually experience the learning activity. The group reconvenes for discussion in order that ideas from the

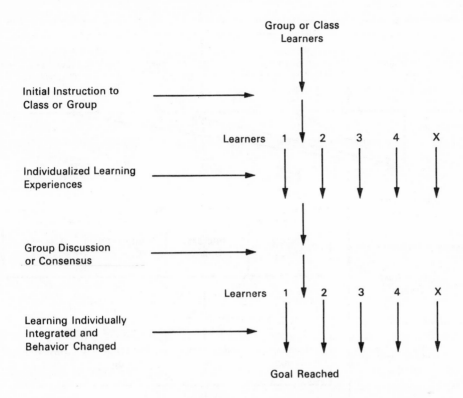

FIGURE 4–1. *Combining Grouping and Individualizing Activities*

entire group may be applied to the problem. The learners must again separate and each pupil must integrate the learning experience; thereby, behavior is changed and the goal for instruction is reached. (See Figure 4–1.)

Group Flexibility

It is conceivable that a child could be with different children in each group to which he belongs. A pupil could be with one group of children in the achievement group, different children in the special need group, still others in the interest group, research group, and the team group. (See Figure 4–2.)

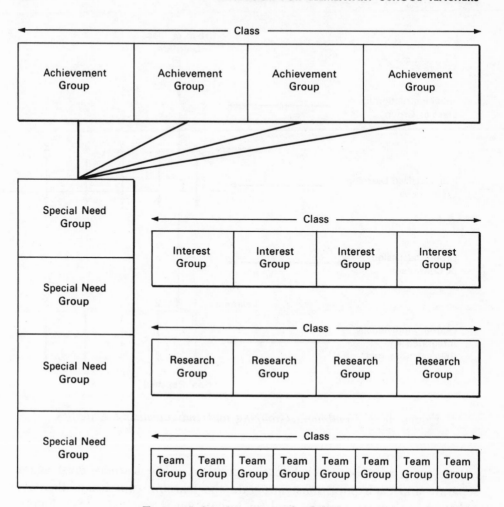

FIGURE 4–2. *Grouping Flexibility*

5

CLASSROOM MANAGEMENT

Familiarity with the subject matter and a knowledge of the latest methods of teaching are not all that will be demanded of an elementary schoolteacher. In fact, other responsibilities seem to require much of his attention, such as keeping accurate attendance records, collecting the lunch money, maintaining a neat and attractive classroom, arranging areas within the room, and distributing and collecting materials.

A teacher who considers himself a professional individual may feel that these tasks are menial and possibly unpleasant, but these responsibilities do exist and must be performed. To ignore these tasks would bring chaos and unhappiness into the class environment. Good classroom management will provide more opportunities to teach and a better environment in which children can learn.

FUNDAMENTAL PROPERTIES

Classroom management is essential for an excellent learning environment. Have you ever noticed that children will always choose the longest crayon or pencil, the cleanest or wrinkle-free sheet of paper, and the newest looking book from the shelf? Children, as well as adults, appreciate beauty and newness surrounding them. A teacher must recognize the necessity of a well-managed classroom and try to provide one that is attractive and comfortable. In addition to these factors, the teacher must encourage classroom courtesy, provide for emergency situations, and establish organizational procedures in order that the classroom will be a place for learning.

A Place to Learn

The classroom is an environment in which a child spends many hours each day. The purpose of schools and classrooms is to facilitate learning. Whether or not this purpose is achieved depends on a number of variables which the teacher can control.

An interesting and eventful classroom is one variable which the teacher can manipulate. This type of a classroom would exhibit contrast and variety. For example, the bulletin boards could reflect ongoing activities within the classroom, yet they could display variety. Representative samples of children's art work would also produce contrast. Centers of interest for reading, science, and social studies also make the classroom more eventful for the children.

A second variable for a place to learn is that the classroom must involve the children in the environment. The classroom should attract the children to it. The pictures, plants, animals, and library corner should stimulate children's questions, curiosity or a need to learn. In order to attract children, the room need not be a work of art, but the bulletin boards should be uncluttered, closet and cupboard doors should be closed, torn books should be mended, pictures without ragged edges should be displayed, and the room should be clean and neat.

The place for a child to learn would be an environment which informs children. This third variable, if applied by the teacher, would subtly instruct the child. Applying printed labels to various objects in the first grade classroom would be an example of the environment informing the child. Other examples are placing compass directions on the walls or marking feet and inches on the floor.

Physical Comfort

Ventilation and heating are fundamental properties for good classroom management; they should be a major concern of the teacher. For most activities in the classroom a temperature of sixty-eight to seventy degrees is suitable. The room should not be allowed to become stuffy or too warm. Make sure that there is enough air movement to carry away unpleasant odors and that a fresh supply of air is readily available.

It is important that sufficient lighting be maintained in all areas of the room.

The teacher should arrange the various interest centers, tables, desks, and working areas so that glare from chalkboards, furniture, and other surfaces will be avoided. Window shades should be adjusted for proper lighting to avoid glare for the pupils who may be seated near the windows; hence, artificial lighting is essential in many areas of the classroom.

Classroom Courtesy

Through the teacher's example, classroom courtesy and politeness may be taught. The teacher who displays a courteous attitude toward his students is encouraging them to be courteous, not only to the teacher but to others in the room.

If the teacher learns each child's name as soon as possible, this will also add to classroom control and courtesy. The teacher should address the children in a kindly, respectful manner and he should insist that the children should address him in a like manner.

Classroom courtesy should be extended to visitors to the room. Many teachers appoint children to welcome guests and to assist the guests in finding a place to sit as well as materials or books so that they may follow the particular activity which is in progress.

Outdoors to Indoors Adjustment

When children return to the classroom in the morning, after recess or the noon lunch period, a teacher should provide a period of time for adjustment. Usually this adjustment period may be only five minutes. A teacher who does not plan for outdoor to indoor adjustment may find her lesson plan objectives not reached because the children are not ready to begin.

During these few minutes, many different activities may be planned. In the morning during roll call and lunch money accounting, the teacher could provide for a class sharing time, a current event reporting period or a library book free reading period. After recess a musical record may be played or a beautiful picture may be discussed. After the lunch period possibly the teacher could provide for the younger children to rest by placing their heads on the table or desk. Another activity which all children seem to enjoy following the noon period is for the teacher to read orally to the children from their favorite story books.

ORGANIZATION

Classroom organization is another very important facet to good classroom management. Such a mundane task as the arrangement of the tables, desks, and other furniture in the room can have an effect on a child's behavior. If a simple task as furniture arrangement affects children, then classroom organization becomes even more important for the teacher to consider. Organizational activities such as seating arrangements, attendance and lunch collection, rules and regulations, pupil movement, and a place in the room for learning and teaching devices are a few of the problems a teacher much be willing to solve.

Seating Arrangements

Children in the primary grades (especially first grade) should have their chairs or desks arranged in such a way that they do not see another child's manuscript writing, number activity or other school work upside down. Many children in the primary grades exhibit orientation problems and some even have difficulty in left-to-right direction. Comparing their work with the child sitting across the table would compound the orientation problem a child may have.

In the middle and upper grades, seating arrangements could be such that children can see each other's face instead of the back of his head. A few children in these grades ,could have orientation problems but it is not as crucial in these grades as the primary grades.

A pupil should have his desk or table and chair adjusted to fit his size and physique. His feet, for instance, should rest comfortably on the floor when seated. The desk or table should not be too high or too low for comfortable table top work.

Inasmuch as the learner is an active individual, adequate orderly space is needed in the classroom for each child. There should be an open area for dramatizing a story, demonstrating a science project or other activity. The room needs to be arranged so that there are adequate spaces for movement within the classroom and several interest areas. Traffic lanes in and out of the room should be kept free and open. An orderly arranged classroom seems to have an orderly effect upon children within that room.

Attendance and Lunch Collection

Poor management on the part of a teacher during the roll call or the collection of lunch money will cause poor behavioral problems in the classroom. As stated earlier in this chapter, this time should be planned for the children. This gives a child an opportunity to share something with the class, report briefly a current event or time to do pleasurable reading. The taking of the class roll or the collection of lunch money can be handled efficiently with a minimum of class time expended.

There are several methods a teacher could employ to make this task efficient. He could appoint attendance monitors for a row, a group of tables or a certain section of the classroom. These monitors could make a written or oral report of the children that are absent. The use of a seating chart would also aid in taking an attendance record. By noting the empty desks and comparing them with the seating chart, this task would be handled in a minimum of time. These routine tasks of taking attendance and accounting for children who will be eating in the school cafeteria could be assumed by children, thus freeing the teacher for more important tasks.

Rules and Regulations

The teacher should seek to achieve an attitude of informality and freedom within his classroom which will assist the learning environment; however, rules and regulations are essential to protect the individual child against intrusions into his process of learning. A sufficient amount of rules and regulations are necessary in order to avoid wasted time and energy. Although the precise number and nature of these rules and regulations will vary from one classroom to another, they should be as few and as uncomplicated as possible.

Children should assist the teacher in making the rules and regulations. At a class meeting, the pupils *guided* by the teacher could set up the rules and regulations to be followed. When the children are involved and have a voice in making the rules, there seems to be less dissenters. The children also learn some important lessons about classroom democracy. Once the rules and regulations are developed, the teacher should be consistent in enforcing them.

Pupil Movement

Some teachers have rather strict regulations about pupils wandering around the school and classroom. Other teachers find that it is not necessary. It seems that the best approach is to use different forms of permissions to suit the occasion. For example, the teacher may give permission to the children in the classroom to sharpen their pencils or place paper in the wastebasket at any convenient time, but to leave the classroom, a child must request permission each and every time he leaves.

Problems that can result when children are moving about the classroom can be eliminated before they exist if the teacher is constantly aware of each child at all times. To be aware of each child, the teacher must look every few minutes about the classroom, account for each child, see what he is doing, and determine if he is approaching an individual crisis. At first, the teacher must constantly and consistently force himself to break away from the ongoing activity and check on the children. Later, however, this procedure will become a good habitual response. If the teacher is alert at all times to what is happening in the classroom, he is prepared to give extra help at a trouble spot and thus eliminate a behavioral problem.

Place for Everything

Every teacher should avoid having to waste his time or the pupils' time searching for equipment and materials. All classroom equipment, supplies, and teaching devices should be kept in a specific place. Anyone who uses these items should be responsible for their return to the proper place when he finishes using them.

Classroom drawers and closets also should be kept in order. A well-ordered closet or drawer makes it easily accessible to select and return teaching equipment. A simple procedure to follow is to have the shelves in the drawers and closets labeled so as to identify the objects to be placed on each.

MATERIALS COLLECTION AND DISTRIBUTION

In addition to organizational abilities, the teacher should also be a manager of the materials within his classroom. Materials collection, distribution, and preparation are all necessarily planned activities in which the teacher must be involved. Not only must he be concerned about these planned activities, but he must also provide for library and reference materials and other learning aids in the well-managed classroom.

Materials Preparation

Materials that are necessary for the day's activity should be prepared and ready for use at the time in which the activity begins. Children waiting for materials could create many behavioral problems. Not only do the children become impatient, but they may lose interest in the project if the materials are not ready.

The teacher should not have just the minimum quantities of materials on hand; some extra materials should be available in case they are needed. Problems arise when children make a mistake and need to start over. It is apparent that the teacher should plan ahead and be ready for any type of an emergency.

Distribution and Collection of Materials

Much of the teacher's time and energy can be saved if books, materials, and supplies are distributed in a business-like preplanned system. Children can be assigned to distribute certain books or materials at the proper time. If classroom drawers and supply closets are kept in excellent order, the children will be able to get the materials quickly. The same children who distributed the materials could collect them and return them to the proper places in drawers, shelves or closets.

When written papers are to be collected, the teacher could select a child from each row, table or specific area of the classroom to gather these papers for him. This takes a very little time and eliminates the noisy confusion that results when papers are handed up the row or around the table from one child to another. Some pupils, as they pass the written papers, stop to compare answers or other children's work and delay the collection of papers.

Library and Reference Materials

The teacher should provide library books and reference materials in his classroom. Many public libraries, as well as the school library, will allow large quantities of books to be checked out by the teacher at one time for classroom use. These books should be rotated every few weeks. Dictionaries and reference books as well as maps, globes, and other learning materials should be readily accessible.

VALUES

Appropriate classroom management conditions the behavior in the school.

Proper classroom management frees the teacher and the pupils for teaching-learning activities.

An orderly and well-managed classroom environment encourages children to spend their energies in study and learning.

Classroom organization provides freedom and informality within the classroom; this is conducive to creating interested and active children in the learning process.

LIMITATIONS AND PROBLEMS

Many teachers consider classroom management problems as menial and *least* important in planning. Thus, they do not organize and manage their classrooms.

Classroom management may become so routinized that humanizing of the curriculum and identity of the individual child are lost.

Rules and regulations may be proliferated to the extent that the teacher may spend his entire time in this area rather than in creating a learning environment.

ILLUSTRATED CLASSROOM ARRANGEMENTS

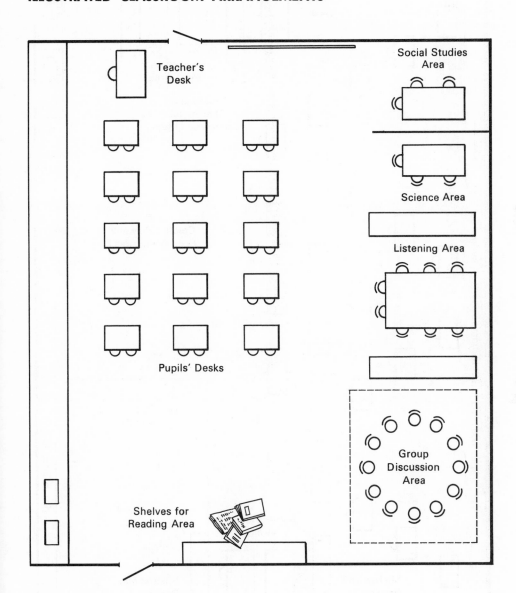

FIGURE 5–1. *Room Arrangement for a Primary, Middle or Upper Grade Classroom*

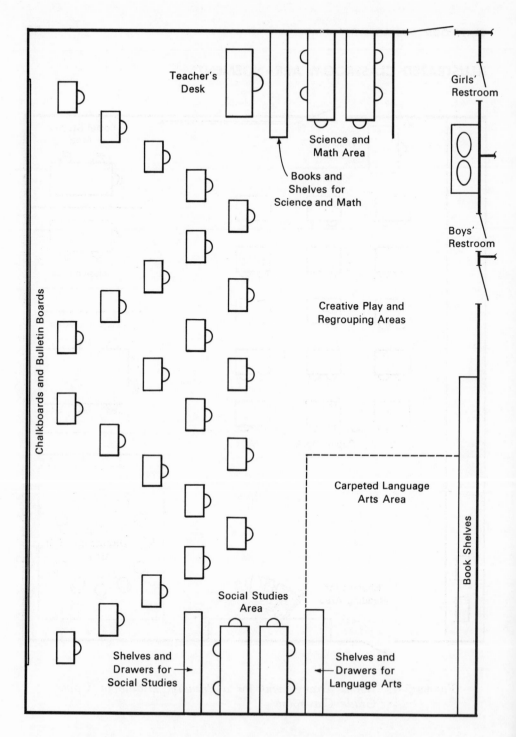

FIGURE 5–2. *Room Arrangement for a Primary Grade Classroom*

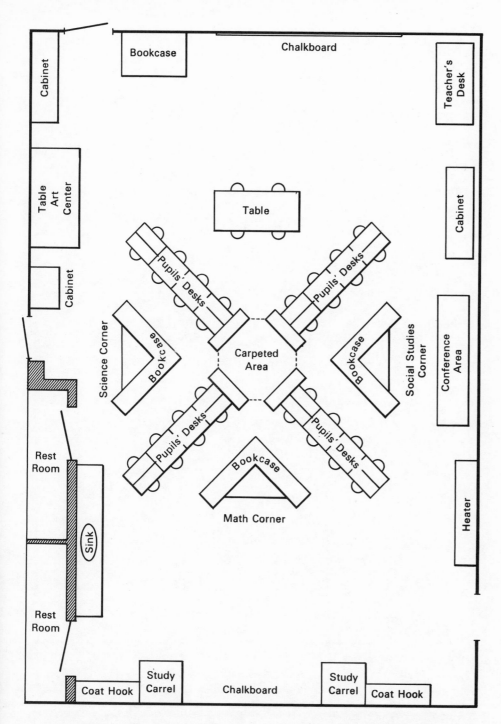

Cabinet

Bookcase

Chalkboard

Teacher's Desk

Table
Art
Center

Cabinet

Cabinet

Table

Pupils' Desks

Pupils' Desks

Science Corner

Bookcase

Carpeted Area

Bookcase

Social Studies Corner

Conference Area

Rest Room

Pupils' Desks

Pupils' Desks

Sink

Bookcase

Math Corner

Heater

Rest Room

Coat Hook

Study Carrel

Chalkboard

Study Carrel

Coat Hook

FIGURE 5–3. *Room Arrangement for a Middle or Upper Grade Classroom*

6

CLASSROOM DISCIPLINE
AND BEHAVIOR

One of the most difficult tasks of teaching is to establish and maintain order in the classroom. Few hours go by without some behavior incident, be it large or small, which needs a teacher's attention. All teachers of children have discipline problems.

Teachers must help pupils develop a desire to learn. Learning in today's schools, however, occurs in a social setting. Classrooms are crowded; individuals from all walks of life are thrown together; interests, abilities, and achievement vary tremendously within each class group. Such factors necessarily create problems of classroom order. Thus, the desire to learn must be carefully guided in such a way as to create optimum conditions for all. It is not too difficult to discover and evolve discipline techniques which work for the moment. It is more difficult to develop techniques which will eventuate into *self*-discipline. Nevertheless, this is the aim of effective teaching.

FUNDAMENTAL PROPERTIES

The word *discipline* is apparently derived from the root word *disciple*, which means to follow or study under an accepted leader. In early civilization, discipline implied teaching or helping one to grow or achieve. Later it became associated with blind conformity. Today it means many things to many people. It is probably the most talked about but least understood of all problems of teaching.

The aim of good discipline is to help the individual adjust to the personal and social *forces* of his experiences. First, the child must learn to adjust to himself as a growing and developing individual. Second, the child must adjust to the existing culture and institutions within which he participates. Finally, he often will have to adjust standards of his home environment to those of the school. The problem of discipline today consists mainly of helping the child develop disciplined and acceptable inner controls.

There are several variables or properties that may cause behavioral problems. These variables can be classified into three broad categories, as follows:

1. Teacher-caused problems
2. Pupil-caused problems
3. School-situation caused problems

Teacher-Caused Problems

Many discipline problems are teacher-caused, such as the following:

1. Inappropriate activity for the time of day or circumstances
2. Sarcasm
3. Inconsistency
4. Being impolite and inconsiderate
5. Having favorites
6. Gossiping about pupils in public places
7. Failure to make class and lesson purposes clear to pupils
8. Using the same method day after day
9. Failure to provide for individual differences
10. Talking "over" noise
11. A classroom which is either too hot or too cold
12. Taking time out for calling roll, taking lunch money, and the like
13. Confusion resulting from disruption of class routines
14. Vague assignments
15. Emphasizing factual-type tests

Pupil-Caused Problems

A second variable contributing to disorder within a classroom can be considered pupil-caused. Pupils usually are quick to exploit an unfortunate situation. Some of them dislike school and most teachers associated with it. Others, just like all human beings, react in terms of health, emotions, and passing interests. Certainly the home, family, and culture of the child can also affect his perception of the school and his classroom. The child's perceptions can ultimately establish priorities, values and needs for learning which can contribute to pupil-caused disorders in the classroom. A number of pupil-caused situations which tend to contribute to possible disorder in the classroom are:

1. The child who "clowns" for attention in the classroom
2. The child from an emotionally unsound home
3. The child who is sick
4. The child who does not have space to do school work at home
5. The child who watches TV all night
6. The child who lacks reading skills needed for an assignment
7. The child who comes from a culture that feels it is "sissy" to read or go to school

School-Situation Caused Problems

A typical elementary school may have all kinds of activities which disrupt the school day, such as the following:

1. The last few minutes of the day
2. The last few minutes prior to lunch
3. The last few minutes of the day on Friday
4. The first part of the class following recess or fire drill
5. Before a holiday or classroom party
6. The first few days of school
7. Appearance of a substitute teacher
8. The last few days of school
9. Inflexible schedules
10. Disruptive announcements over the public address system
11. Unregulated visitor behavior
12. Poorly planned school activities schedules

13. Poor lighting and ventilation
14. Food smells from the cafeteria
15. Band and chorus practice next door

DEVELOPMENT OF DISCIPLINE WITHIN CHILDREN

Discipline is hard for children to learn because it is composed of innumerable specifics. Truth, honesty, dependability, respect for property, privacy, personality, helpfulness to others, and protection of smaller people are just a few of the rules of society that each new generation must learn to uphold. Some children learn such lessons at home and need only *apply* them at school. Others must *learn* the rules of the game. The acquisition and alteration of attitudes and values take time. Patience is essential. One's teaching task in discipline is similar to his task in any other field. Children learn some things by listening, but they are more likely to remember and act on their *own words and ideas.* They need to solve their own problems—to make proposals, seek out and analyze the available data, test their own hypotheses, and examine their own results.

Children will learn more quickly if they are permitted to assist in setting up their own rules of conduct. However, the teacher must retain the right to determine what action is needed when rules are broken. This is made necessary because behavior results from many *different* causes. The action to be taken must be determined by the cause(s) and the individual involved. For instance, a class may decide that late assignments should not count as much as those turned in on time. There are times, however, when such action would be most inappropriate (sickness, special emergencies, etc.). The teacher must weigh each case separately.

How does one respond to misbehavior of stable children? First he must determine the cause(s). If the teacher decides that the individual does not yet know or understand what is expected, he should *talk, discuss, and explain.* This is effective at times; however, the problem may need more action than discussion and explanation.

Punishment and reward may be necessary at other times—both are effective and both are appropriate techniques to use. Whenever possible, though, reward (the positive approach) should be used. Punishment causes one to remember because of pain, discomfort or fear, whereas reward gives pleasure or satisfaction.

GUIDELINES FOR HANDLING CLASS DISTURBANCES

There are a number of general guidelines which many teachers have found to be effective. However, the reader is cautioned against assuming any fixed procedure in class disturbances.

Disturbing conversation. Sometimes such a disturbance can be ignored. If it threatens to spread, the teacher can move to the area of disturbance. He may offer to help the pupils get started on an assignment. If the teacher is talking to the entire group, a pause or a question to one of the disturbing pupils can effectively solve the problem. Although some teachers are quick to separate pupils who disturb, this is often an inadvisable procedure. The practice may create resentment and serve to spread the problem to other parts of the room.

Passing notes. Such activities are symptomatic of a boring experience or lack of appropriate challenge. Frequently a change of pace takes care of the situation. It is not appropriate to read notes aloud to the class.

Over-dependence of one child on another. This is a problem which usually will work itself out. The pupils sometimes need each other until wider social acceptance is possible. Wider social acceptance is encouraged through emphasis on group work in which pupils are grouped sociometrically.

Hostility between individuals and/or groups. Talk with each of the participants individually. Try to find the cause prior to any drastic attempts at reformation.

Cheating. Cheating may occur as a result of overemphasis on grades or the establishment of unrealistic standards. In Chapter 4, on individual differences, the importance of making assignments and tests commensurate with pupils' abilities was emphasized. If the task is too hard for the person he will be forced to cheat in order to meet the requirement.

Tattletales. Children should be taught the difference between tattletales and reporting. A tattletale is one who tells *personal* things, whereas a child who *reports* about another child has been given the responsibility to do so because the child being reported is breaking a *school or classroom rule.* Children need to learn and be helped to distinguish between tattling as a busybody operation and reporting as an essential group function. Tattling deals with the insignificant; reporting deals with consequential information regarding the health, safety, and welfare of the children in the class and with a particular classroom routine or regulation essential to effective classroom operation. Teachers need to treat tattling and reporting with consistency. Younger children need many opportunities to consider the subtle differences between these two items.

Temper tantrum. When a child in the classroom has a temper tantrum everyone in the classroom should avoid giving the child an audience. The teacher should move the child to the pupil's desk or table, or the teacher may need to remove him from the classroom altogether so other children will not give him an audience. The teacher may find out what caused the child to have a temper tantrum and then try to help the child to see his behavior in a different way. This may prevent it from happening again.

Refusal to comply with a teacher request. Sometimes a teacher makes a simple request, only to discover that the child refuses to obey. What should be done under the circumstances? The action to be taken will, of course, depend upon the nature of the request. Refusal to comply with simple requests usually is associated with high emotional tension. Don't argue with the child, continued argumentative dialogue makes things worse. Don't make statements or threats which cannot be enforced or which give the teacher or the child no alternatives for subsequent behavior. Usually the teacher can take the child by the hand and direct him toward that which was requested; however, it may be necessary to take the child from the room and discuss the problem with the child. It is very important, however, that teacher requests be followed. Failure to comply should be subject to certain consequences. Unreasonable requests should be avoided. A reasonable request for one pupil may be unreasonable for another. Provide a cooling-off, reflective period to allow both child and teacher to reduce emotional levels and to become more objective; then the problem may be more easily handled by both teacher and pupil.

Isolation. Separating a child from his peers tends to reinforce the craving which induced the behavior in the first place. It may be necessary to isolate a pupil *temporarily* as a stopgap measure, but continued use of this technique can only lead to greater frustration, and deeper feelings of guilt, and resentment.

Removal from the situation. While there will be times when a child must be removed from the classroom, it should be used only as a last resort. In such instances the teacher is admitting his inability to handle the situation. When it becomes necessary the offender should be sent to a specific member of the teaching or administrative staff. In other words, he should not be sent from the room without adequate provisions for supervision.

VALUES

Appropriate classroom activities will cause good behavior.

Proper control and assistance will help the child to operate ultimately under his own initiative and direction.

Positive motivation will decrease discipline problems. A close relationship between motivation and discipline is evident.

The individual child's well-being will be enhanced through good practices in discipline. Techniques of discipline will be varied for each individual in the classroom.

Good discipline will help the child adjust to the personal and social forces of his experiences.

LIMITATIONS AND PROBLEMS

Discipline problems probably are the most subtle and least understood in all aspects of teaching.

Teachers assume that that disciplinary measure which seems reasonable to them should appear reasonable to children.

Poor behavior is caused.

The mere process of keeping pupils busy and orderly is not enough.

Consistency on the part of the teacher in handling discipline problems is difficult to maintain.

ILLUSTRATIONS

Discipline and Motivation Guidelines

The principles which follow are basic to the problem of discipline. Guiding principles for effective motivation are essentially the same for effective discipline.

1. Reward is more effective than punishment.
2. Motivation which originates with the individual is more effective than that which is imposed from without.

3. Immediate reinforcement of a desirable response is needed.
4. Motivation is contagious, that is, a highly interested and motivated teacher tends to produce highly interested and motivated pupils.
5. A clear understanding of purpose enhances motivation.
6. All children have certain psychological needs which must be met.
7. Self-imposed tasks tend to create more interest than do teacher-imposed tasks.
8. "External" rewards sometimes are necessary and effective in stimulating initial interest.
9. Varied teaching techniques and procedures are effective in maintaining interest.
10. It is economical to capitalize on existing interests.
11. Activities which stimulate interest for the less able may be inappropriate for the more able, and vice versa.
12. High anxiety makes learning difficult or impossible.
13. Anxiety and frustration in mild form can be beneficial to learning.
14. If the task is too difficult and if assistance is not readily available, frustration quickly leads to demoralization.
15. Each pupil has a different level of frustration tolerance.
16. Peer group pressure is much more effective in discipline than adult-imposed pressures.
17. All human beings need and expect the imposition of reasonable limits to guide their conduct.

7

QUESTIONING TECHNIQUES

Questioning is the heart of teaching. It is involved in some way with every method described in this book. Indeed one might say that a teacher is (or should be) a professional question maker. Asking questions is one of the most effective means of stimulating thinking and learning. This chapter provides assistance in questioning techniques.

FUNDAMENTAL PROPERTIES

Instructional goals, as described in Chapter 2, are designed to emphasize critical thinking. Consequently, each instructional method is developed within a framework of critical thinking processes. Critical thinking may be conceived as including all thought processes beyond the memory level. Thus it seems appropriate to treat questions from the vantage point of *levels*. Recall, comprehension, analysis and evaluation provide such a frame of reference.

Recall Questions

Factual questions often involve the key words of "who," "what," "when," and "where." There is but one correct answer. The pupil is required merely to recall or recognize information. The category includes recall of facts such as dates, events, persons, and places. Also included is *recall* of basic principles and generalizations.

Obviously such information is needed but too often, teachers never expect students to go beyond this level. The greatest problem involves determining what knowledge is worth remembering and how to structure learning around this so that it becomes a means rather than the end of instruction.

Though the recall of specific facts is essential to all levels of thinking, it must be remembered that unrelated facts are quickly forgotten. Moreover, memorized knowledge may not represent a very high level of understanding. Above all, concentrating on memory neglects other intellectual processes learned through practice. Solving problems is learned by actual practice rather than by memorizing the inductive conclusions derived by others.

Comprehension Questions

After the learner gives evidence that he has the essential facts well in hand, questions to determine *understanding* are asked. Comprehension questions characteristically require the learner to *manipulate* information. He must relate facts, generalizations, and definitions by bringing in relationships between ideas. Key words in this category are "how" and "why." Whereas recall questions call for remembering, comprehension questions call for manipulation and modification in some way. To illustrate:

1. What factors contributed to the Westward Movement in 1800's? (Involves recall of text materials.)
2. Why did the pioneers seek new lands? (Involves an understanding.)

Although the foregoing illustrations appear to be characteristic of the two levels cited, the first question could be comprehensive in nature if the pupil must draw inferences from various media sources. If, however, the answer is to be found in the textbook or if the information has been previously presented in the classroom or in a report, the question is merely one of recall. Likewise, the second question may be a memory item if the answer has been previously given to the pupil. Thus the *conditions of a question* must be known before it can be accurately classified. Question classification is a tool for recognizing the thought processes involved in answering them. For convenience, application-type questions are included as a form of comprehension. The same kind of reasoning is involved except that the pupil is not informed relative to the specific idea or concept to be applied.

Comprehension questions may be subdivided into four groups: interpretation, summarization, example, and definition. The first of these, illustrated above, asks the pupil to show relationships between facts or ideas. He may show likenesses, differences, cause and effect relationships or comparisons. Summarization merely requires the pupil to restate ideas in his own words. Examples call for an illustration of the idea involved. Finally, the pupil may be expected to formulate his own definition of some idea. (It cannot be one that has already been given.)

A major element of questioning tactics is knowing when and how to introduce higher order questions. For example, a comprehension question may elicit a recall response or perhaps a personal reaction. In such cases the teacher should probe for the analysis expected. Thus, a series of questions may be initiated.

Analysis Questions

The process of analysis involves taking apart information and making relationships. The purpose is to clarify by discovering hidden meaning and basic structure. The pupil is able to read between the lines, to distinguish between fact and opinion, to assess the degree of consistency or inconsistency. In science, for example, the pupil is able to distinguish between relevant and extraneous materials or events. Likewise, in the social studies area, a pupil is able to detect unstated assumptions.

Whereas comprehension questions emphasize *understanding*, analysis questions *involve seeking out underlying relationships and organizational patterns*. Certain key words suggest analysis. Among these are assumptions, motives, implications, identification of issues, logical fallacies, and processes of induction and deduction. Analysis questions ask the pupil to solve a problem by conscious observance of *established criteria*.

It should be emphasized that analysis questions follow questions of comprehension. The reader will recall the comprehension question cited earlier: "Why did the pioneers seek new lands?" An analysis question could then be asked: "What *implications* can be drawn concerning their old farm lands?" (This assumes that the available implications have not been drawn by others.) As a general rule, analysis questions require the pupil to detect a logic or relationship between variables. The hidden motives, assumptions, and implications are not the product of wild or even individual speculation, however. They follow established rules of logic and must be consistent with the known facts.

Evaluation Questions

It should be noted that the Bloom taxonomy makes two distinct categories that are included here under evaluation. These categories are labeled synthesis and evaluation. Synthesis is seen as a process of reassembly for new meaning. Thus the learner may develop new or creative ideas—ideas which were not apparent previous to this time. At this point in the critical thinking process he offers proposals for solving the problem under consideration. Closely related is evaluation in which the learner critically examines the proposals offered through analysis. Evaluation may be deferred as in the case when the objective is to generate as many ideas as possible. Frequently, however, evaluation follows immediately after an idea is proposed. Often this is accomplished in a *single pupil response*. For this reason the processes of synthesis and evaluation are treated as a single aspect of questioning technique.

Evaluation questions call for comments involving judgments, opinions, personal reactions, and criticisms. Responses are judged on the basis of stated criteria. These criteria may be imposed by the questioner or they may be advanced by the respondent. Such questions usually include or imply such key words as "should," "could" or "would." Questions such as "In your opinion . . .", "What is your personal reaction . . .", "How would you evaluate . . .", "Do you think . . .", tend to call for evaluations. Unless otherwise indicated, the pupil should state his opinion and then provide a basis for such views. It becomes apparent that there is no one right or wrong answer to such questions. Answers are judged on the basis of how well the response was defended. Sometimes a teacher may ask a pupil to state his views from a given frame of reference. In such cases the views are defended and judged on the basis of the given framework. "If you had an opportunity to move West with the pioneers, *what do you think* would be the problems you would face?" In this case the pupil would be expected to *state and support* his views. The question could be stated in another way, however. "If you could have moved West with the pioneers, how would the Indians affect your journey?" In this case the answer must be defended from a provided frame of reference.

Evaluation questions involve both the intellectual and the emotional aspects of learning. Accordingly, some responses will tend to be highly biased and opinionated. While this is to be expected on occasion, continued emphasis on acceptable criteria is needed.

Problem Questions

Although evaluation questions are considered to represent the highest order of complexity, some attention should be directed to those problem questions used as a starting point for most instructional methods. The various methods treated in subsequent chapters are developed within a broad framework of critical thinking or problem solving. Those which embody the entire problem-solving process are developed from broad problems of policy. A problem of policy is an open-ended question which implies a needed change from the *status quo*. Often it begins with the word "what" but may begin with such key words as "why" or "how." The words "should" or "ought" also are stated or implied in the question. For example, "What action should be taken to keep the school yard cleaner?" It is assumed (by the wording of the question) that some further action is needed.

A problem of policy is treated most effectively when certain definable steps are followed. Each instructional method has its own unique problem-solving approach. Each level of questioning, previously described, usually will be employed. To illustrate from the above example:

1. What have we done to keep the school yard clean? (Recall question)
2. Why is it necessary to keep the school yard clean? (Comprehension question)
3. What are the benefits of a clean school yard relative to us in the school? (Analysis question)
4. In your judgment, how has keeping the school yard clean helped us? (Evaluation question)

It should be noted that several or even all the questioning levels may be employed in each phase of the problem-solving process. Greater emphasis will be placed on certain questions at each level, however. For example, during the earlier part of a discussion recall questions will receive considerable emphasis.

Problem questions must be carefully preplanned. If such questions are ill-conceived, the subsequent problem-solving experience is of limited value. The most common error results from confusion between certain types of evaluation questions and questions of policy. An evaluation question, in effect, tends to deal with one possible solution to a problem, whereas a policy question opens the door to any number of possible solutions. In the foregoing illustration, for example, one possible solution could be to make each class of pupils clean up and police the school yard by their room. Sometimes the teacher, due to his own advance understanding and/or existing biases, may word the problem as an evaluation-type question. To illustrate: "Should each class of pupils clean up around their own room?" Under such conditions, discussion tends to be limited to the merits and limitations of the one proposal.

ENHANCING PUPIL ANSWERS

An understanding of question levels is but a small part of the art of questioning. As previously indicated, questioning techniques are directly or indirectly associated with all the "logical operations" of teaching.

Probing for Answers

Probing for more adequate answers is a well-known but often neglected technique. Socrates, who lived in the fourth century B.C., became famous for his skill in eliciting correct responses through probing procedures which involves a question or a series of questions addressed to the *same* pupil. It is used when an initial response is inadequate. There are two principle types of probing—prompting and clarification.

Prompting involves the use of short hints or clues when the pupil is unable to give an answer or gives an incorrect answer to a question. Prior to the prompting sequence it may be desirable to rephrase the question to be certain that the pupil understands what is being sought. Prompting involves a series of questions designed to elicit those things the pupil knows relative to the original question. Thus the procedure usually involves a series of *recall* questions, designed to lead the pupil back to the original question. The procedure is used when the pupil is suspected of possessing the necessary background knowledge for handling the question. It is designed to guide him in the critical thinking processes. To illustrate:

T: How does the principle of immunization work?

P: I don't know.

T: Using a smallpox vaccination as an example, what happens if the vaccination "takes"? (A different question, recall in nature)

P: He usually gets sick and has a high temperature.

T: Good. Are there any other problems? (Recall question)

P: He develops a sore at the place of the vaccination.

T: Fine. Now what does this suggest to you about smallpox? (Comprehension question)

P: If he had smallpox, he would have these sores all over his body; so I guess the one sore is a little bit of the disease.

T: Your answer is basically correct. Why is an individual made immune to the disease? (Analysis question)

P: His body, with the one sore, builds up defenses against the disease.

As the illustration suggests, the pupil is not told that his answer is wrong. Instead he is encouraged or reinforced at every step along the way. This tends to help him build confidence in himself. Generally one should avoid interpreting or rephrasing the pupil's response. All too often a teacher will inappropriately pass on to another pupil if an answer is not immediately forthcoming. This tends to cut such an individual out of the discussion. In some cases about 10 percent of a class may make 90 percent of the contributions.

Clarification is a probing technique which calls for a restatement or expansion of a response. Usually it is sought when the response is not incorrect but still does not measure up to the teacher's expectations. Instead of giving hints, the pupil is asked to improve his response. Such comments as the following are often used: "Explain"; "Would you restate your answer in another way?"; "What else can you add?"; "Are there other reasons?"

T: What happens in the body when a person is immunized?

P: Well, we are usually immunized against such diseases as smallpox and measles.

T: These are good examples but what actually happens in the body when we are immunized against such diseases?

It may be necessary to do some prompting if the pupil is unable to clarify his original response satisfactorily.

EFFECTIVE TECHNIQUES IN QUESTIONING

Most teachers and certainly pupils recognize that the teacher and a few individuals tend to do most of the talking in class. Although there are many psychological forces at work in any given class, there are certain techniques which may greatly reduce teacher talk and expand the number of participating pupils.

The most obvious technique is the practice of calling on *non-volunteers*. When pupils realize that they are not likely to be called upon unless their hands are raised, they are likely to keep their hands down. The few pupils who do raise their hands tend to monopolize the experience. Usually, they are the ones who have a good grasp of the problem and who like the reinforcement provided. The teacher, in turn, is reinforced by the apparent group progress suggested by his volunteer respondents. Non-volunteers, however, most need the experience of active participation. Pupil participation is enhanced when both volunteers and non-volunteers are asked to respond. The teacher can simply announce that he will call upon individuals whether their hands are raised or not.

Another effective technique to enhance questioning effectiveness is through *redirection*. Teacher talk can be minimized by asking questions which elicit several responses. This may involve a question in which several "reasons" or "factors" may be requested, or it may be one in which differences of opinion exist. Thus different pupils are expected to offer "reasons" or "opinions." It may be necessary to cue the group to what is expected by saying, "This question has many parts to it. Please give only one when you answer." Redirection has the added advantage of encouraging pupils to respond to each other. (All too often the pattern is teacher-question-pupil responses, etc.)

Another rather obvious but frequently misused technique is that of stating a question prior to calling upon the individual who is to respond. Not only should this practice be followed but the teacher should pause for a few seconds after he asks the question and before he calls upon someone to provide an answer. If the teacher designates a respondent *prior* to the question, the rest of the class will tend to relax and may not even "hear" the question. By pausing, each pupil is given time to organize his thinking for a thorough answer. Obviously, higher level questions demand a few seconds for meditation.

Still another technique for enhancing question effectiveness is the practice of allowing adequate time for an individual to formulate his response. Some pupils need more time for expression than others. A teacher who habitually cuts a pupil off before he is finished tends to discourage the shy. He should avoid interpreting a pupil's response to fit his own criterion of acceptability. Clarification is in order here. Those pupils who tend to ramble on and on without actually saying what they mean can be encouraged to write out their thoughts before responding verbally.

Too often neglected is the relationship of questions to individual differences. Although dull pupils can handle higher order questions, they cannot be expected to bring in the degree of association expected of bright pupils. Likewise, some pupils tend to be more adept at divergent thinking than others. By adapting questions to the individual, greater attention to different approaches to an issue can be gained.

VALUES

Questioning techniques apply to all instructional methods. The success of any given instructional experience is dependent largely upon how questions are handled.

Critical thinking is encouraged through the artful use of questioning techniques and thought-provoking questions aimed above the level of mere recall.

Questions which call for multiple answers cause a questioning pattern which is most helpful for pupil growth. The questioning pattern may be teacher-question-pupil response, pupil-response, pupil-question-pupil response, etc.

Effective questioning tactics depend upon a climate in which participation is encouraged and answers are reinforced.

Probing techniques enable the individual to judge the adequacy of his own response.

Wide participation is achieved because the teacher calls upon both non-volunteers and volunteers.

Individual differences among pupils in the classroom may be handled in questioning sessions by the effective teacher. Some children can handle thought-provoking questions while others can provide recall answers. Thus, all children may participate and contribute to a discussion.

LIMITATIONS AND PROBLEMS

Teacher behaviors of repeating questions, answering one's own questions, and repeating pupil responses tend to be major obstacles to effective questioning processes.

Many teachers encounter difficulty in developing reflective thought within pupils because of the way they phrase their questions. A question which calls for a "yes" or "no" answer usually discourages discussion.

The foremost problem associated with questioning techniques is the tendency to emphasize recall only.

There is a tendency for teachers to "rush" pupil responses and to expect answers which fit the teacher's preconceived notions.

A common problem among teachers is to involve relatively few pupils in the questioning process.

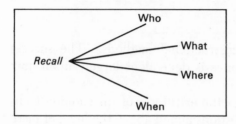 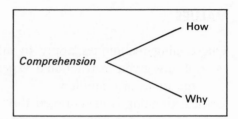

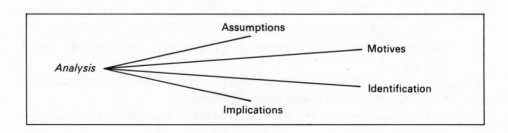

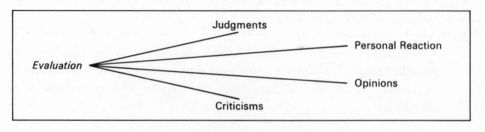

FIGURE 7–1. *Question Levels*

QUESTIONING ILLUSTRATIONS

I. Useful in the reading and language arts areas

A. Comprehension questions
1. Explain Mary's plan to find her dog in the story you just read.
2. How do you know in the story that Tom tried to do his best?
3. Why do standards for discussion sometimes prevent proper sharing in the classroom?
4. How does a study of language skills contribute to an understanding of the English language?

B. Analysis questions
1. What was the author's purpose in writing that story you read?
2. What assumptions are suggested when the writer of the story said, "No one could go down in the cave."?
3. What are the main reasons in establishing punctuation rules for writing?
4. Which are the facts and which are the opinions in that report?

C. Evaluation questions
1. Which of the stories in this unit would you consider to be the best story?
2. What do you think of the character, William Tomet, in the story?
3. In your opinion do the *standards for interviewing* help you to make better interviews?
4. What is your personal reaction to the suggestion that research techniques be used in preparing for class reports.

II. Useful in science and arithmetic areas

A. Comprehension questions
1. Compare the moon, mars, and earth with respect to their sizes.
2. Give an example which suggests our mountains are constantly changing.
3. How would you define a cardinal number?
4. What does the fraction 4/3 mean?

B. Analysis questions
1. How are common respiratory diseases related to weather conditions?

2. What techniques can be used to determine if plants need air?
3. What must you know for that answer to be correct?
4. Which are the facts and which items are irrelevant to the arithmetic story problem?

C. Evaluation questions
1. In your opinion why do you suppose so many people talk so much about the weather?
2. For what reason would you favor a laboratory experiment rather than reading about an experiment done by someone else?
3. Which decimal fraction method would you consider to be better?
4. How would you judge the plausibility of your answer to that arithmetic story problem?

III. Useful in the social studies area

A. Comprehension questions
1. What comparisons can be made between clothing in colonial times and clothing today?
2. What does that political cartoon mean?
3. Explain the need for community helpers.
4. State in your own words the reasons for different types of housing.

B. Analysis questions
1. In the story of Davey Crockett which activities are the facts and which activities are the opinions of the writer?
2. What was the author's purpose in writing those things about Abraham Lincoln?
3. What were some of the motives which influenced the United States government to have people migrate to the Oregon territory?
4. What assumptions seem evident from pleas of the southern states to withdraw from the Union prior to the Civil War?

C. Evaluation questions
1. In your opinion should George Washington's Birthday be celebrated on Monday even though it is not February 22?
2. Of these two rules, which rule will result in the greatest good for the greatest number in our class?
3. What is your personal reaction to the study of South America in our social studies this year?
4. Do you think we should celebrate a Betsy Ross Day?

8

BRAINSTORMING
TECHNIQUES

Brainstorming literally means using the *brain* to *storm* a problem. It is a technique by which a group attempts to find a solution for a specific problem by amassing all the ideas spontaneously contributed by its members. Brainstorming is a technique of applied imagination or creativity.[1]

The precise relationship between creative imagination and problem solving presently is not fully understood. Most writers suggest, however, that too much emphasis on the formal structure of analytical thought processes is detrimental to creative (sometimes called intuitive) thought. Routinized activities of any sort seem to be detrimental to the process. In stressing the complementary nature of the two, Bruner concedes that through "intuitive thinking the individual may arrive at solutions or problems which he would achieve at all, or at best more slowly, through analytic thinking."[2] He points out, however, that ideas reached intuitively must be checked and refined by analytic methods. The procedure described in this chapter enables the learner to exercise considerable creativity within the broad framework of the problem-solving process.

[1] Alex F. Osborn, *Applied Imagination*, 3rd rev. ed. (Charles F. Scribner's Sons, 1963), p. 151.
[2] Jerome Bruner, *The Process of Education* (Cambridge, Mass.: Harvard University Press, 1961), p. 58.

FUNDAMENTAL PROPERTIES

Brainstorming embodies the fundamental aspects of creative thought. An idea is creative when it possesses an element of novelty which can be applied to a given situation. The process includes the ability to produce ideas which are relevant and unusual, to see beyond the immediate situation, and to redefine the problem or some aspect of it. The properties described below are basic to creative thinking. Techniques of brainstorming seem to encourage and nurture many of these concepts.

Originality

The ability to produce unusual ideas, to solve problems in unusual ways, and to use things or situations in an unusual manner is the essence of originality. Sometimes it is viewed as uncommonness of response—the ability to make remote or indirect connections. Such an individual, being skeptical of conventional ideas, is predisposed to the intellectual risks associated with creative discovery.

Persistence

A creative person is usually a persistent individual. He often displays a marked willingness to devote long hours to a given task, including a willingness to schedule his own time. Moreover, such an individual may display a willingness to withstand discomfort, often working under adverse conditions. Above all, the creative person displays a willingness to face failure. Frustrations seem to spur him on to greater effort.

Independence

The creative person is an independent thinker. He looks for the unusual, the unexpected. Indeed he notices things that other people do not, such as colors, textures, and personal reactions. Frequently he may explore ideas for their own sake, toying with them to see where they may lead.

As opposed to the counterconformist who flouts convention because he feels a compulsion to be different, the independent thinker maintains a balance between that of the counterconformist and the conformist. Unlike the conformist, he is open to experience; unlike the counterconformist, he is different because of his greater perceptive ability. He has confidence in the worth of his ideas. Although the creative person is his own greatest critic, he has undying faith in his ideas.

Involvement and Detachment

Once a problem has been identified, the creative person quickly becomes immersed in the area. He reads, notes, discusses, and explores. By finding out what others have done, the creator not only provides himself with materials with which to think, but also becomes acquainted with the difficulties and complexities of the problem.

Once such an individual has become fully immersed in his problem, he becomes detached enough to see the problem in its total perspective. By setting his work aside, the creative person gives his ideas freedom to develop. Thus involvement becomes a means of preparing him for his own creation.

Deferment and Immediacy

While allowing the problem to maintain its freshness, the creative person resists the tendency to judge too soon. He does not accept the first solution which appears but waits to see if a better one comes along. This tendency to defer judgment seems to be an attribute of an open-minded person—one who is unwilling to reach a decision prematurely.

Incubation

The aspect of the creative process which calls for little or no conscious effort is known as incubation. By putting the problem aside temporarily, the creative person allows the unconscious to take over, making various associations and connections which the conscious mind seems to impede.

The incubation period may be long or short, but it must be utilized. It permits the mind to run free; it is a period of purposeful relaxation which may vary from a few minutes to several months.

Illumination

Intuitive thought processes are best characterized by a sudden flash of insight. Perhaps after a long period of frustrated effort the solution to a problem will suddenly appear, often at a time when least expected. This sudden flash of insight may be the fruit of unconscious effort in the form of inner tensions. It may be that the powers of association are enhanced when the mind runs freely on its own. At any rate, the flash usually occurs after a period of incubation when the individual is not actively pursuing his problem. Sleep, above all, helps to encourage illumination.

Verification

Although illumination provides the necessary impetus and direction for solving a problem, it must be checked and verified through conventional objective procedures. Sound judgment must complete the work that imagination has set in progress. Indeed a flash of insight may be partially if not totally unreliable. It may serve merely as a catalyst to liberate the creator from a restricted approach to his problem. Sometimes one flash of inspiration will set off a chain reaction to other such experiences during the process of verification.

BRAINSTORMING PROCEDURE

Basically creativity is an individualized process; but, as with analytical thought, it can be encouraged and enhanced through group ideation processes. Brainstorming techniques have been especially effective in this regard.

Identifying the problem

In preparation for a brainstorming session the leader (a pupil or the teacher) selects a *specific*, as opposed to a general, problem. The problem, How should we behave on a field trip?, is too broad. To narrow the problem two or three subproblems might be formulated:　How should we behave on the bus?　How should we behave going to and from the bus?　How should we behave at the water station?

When the problem has been reduced to its lowest common denominator, the selected subproblem(s) is posed as a concise, definite question. Questions of what, why, where, when, who, and how serve to stimulate ideation on a problem.　For example:　Why is it needed?　Where should it be done?　Who should do it?　How should it be done?

Preparing the Group

New participants need to be conditioned for their initial session.　A warm-up practice session on a simple problem will stimulate the production of ideas.　Primary grade children may need this warm-up practice session each time the brainstorming technique is used.

Leading the Ideation Session

In preparation for the actual brainstorming session, the leader explains and writes out four basic rules which must be faithfully followed:

1. *Criticism is ruled out.*　Adverse judgment of ideas must be withheld until later.
2. *"Freewheeling" is welcomed.*　The wilder the idea the better; it is easier to tame down than to think up.
3. *Quantity is wanted.*　The greater the number of ideas, the more the likelihood of useful ideas.
4. *Combination and improvement are sought.*　In addition to contributing ideas of their own, participants should suggest how ideas of others can be turned into *better* ideas, or how two or more ideas can be joined into still another idea.

Brainstorming must be kept informal, except for a recorder or two who keeps a written record of all ideas produced.　Its function is idea-finding— not to deal with problems which primarily depend upon judgment.

The leader can develop his own list of suggested solutions to the problem. However, they are to be used only for "pump priming," that is, when the flow of ideas slows down. He should also be prepared to suggest leads by way of new categories or classifications which might open up new lines of thought.

The setting for brainstorming should be informal and relaxed. Following a short explanation of the problem, a list of the four basic rules (indicated in the first part of this section) is made plainly visible. These rules should be carefully reviewed again, especially for the primary grade child. The leader explains that he will give a specified signal, like knocking on his desk, when a member violates any of the rules. Only one idea is offered at a time by any individual. The leader especially encourages ideas directly sparked by a previous idea. If several children desire to speak at once, the participants are encouraged to jot down ideas before they are forgotten. Because ideas tend to be contagious and many persons often desire to speak at once, groups of about eight to twelve are best adapted to the technique. Much larger groups, however, have been effective under the direction of expert leaders.

The leader frequently will want to repeat ideas as another spur to creative thinking. His objective is to "milk the group dry of ideas." In addition to opening up new channels of thought, he keeps prodding with, "What else?" "I cannot believe that you have expressed all your ideas." etc. Short, silent periods are to be expected as children cast about for ideas. It is usually in the later stage that the most unique and useful ideas emerge. Most ideation sessions will not exceed fifteen minutes. If the group is large and/or if more than one subproblem needs exploration, two or more subgroups may be utilized.

Utilizing Afterthoughts

In closing the ideation session it is interesting to ascertain the number of ideas produced. This serves to stimulate individuals to think further on the problem. The recorder(s) or teacher can quickly scan the ideas for categories. A glance at the full list usually indicates from five to ten classifications. The leader (a pupil or the teacher) asks the participants to keep the problem on their minds until the next day, when they will be asked for afterthoughts. This can be made as a definite assignment. Such an incubation period sometimes produces some of the most valuable of all the ideas.

Processing Ideas

After all ideas (including afterthoughts) have been assembled, they are screened, edited, and placed in appropriate categories. While this may be done by the entire group, it is usually preferable to utilize a committee of from three to five pupils. Usually the teacher will want to assist in this process. It is desirable to establish a list of criteria for evaluation of ideas. One group established the following:

1. The idea must be stated in a short, clear manner.
2. It should be possible.
3. It should have some element of the unusual, the novel.

The committee or teacher must exercise due caution in the elimination of ideas. Some of the "wildest ideas" may contain elements of imagination which will not be obvious at first glance.

Implementing Ideas

How a group uses the ideas of a brainstorming session is largely dependent upon its purpose. In most class settings such experiences are designed to suggest new and novel ideas for some necessary class activity. For example, the task may involve techniques of oral or written expression in art, literature or music. It may involve novel ways of playing certain games, of memorizing, of doing some chore. It may even deal with certain aspects of human relations, such as how to keep calm when one is made angry. Whatever the purpose may be, ideas must be implemented. This may be accomplished on an individual basis or in subgroups. Sometimes the fruits of various action programs may be shared with the children in the classroom. On other occasions they may be of a private nature and may not be shared with anybody else except the teacher.

Deriving Generalizations

As a culminating experience, the group may draw generalizations based upon various action programs. This enables all members to profit from the experiences of many. Certain experiences may set the stage for the enactment of one or more selected situations for further study and analysis. Dramatic play (described in Chapter 10) has been most useful in this connection.

PLANNING FOR BRAINSTORMING

Although the ideation session is characterized by informality, the entire brainstorming experience must be carefully planned. The following plan indicates one way of stimulating a group to creative activity. Since the creative act is in itself a unique experience to the individual involved, the brainstorming method will take on many different dimensions, depending upon the purpose being served.

LESSON PLAN ILLUSTRATION (language arts area—fifth grade)

Concept: Book reports can be imaginative and interesting.

Problem: What different ways may we make book reports?

Goals: After this lesson the pupil should be able to make different book reports, as evidenced by:

1. The variety of book reports he uses.
2. The use of these ideas in his own book reports.

Lesson Approach:

As has been previously pointed out, book reports can be different from the written type book reports we are using now. Is it necessary to write out the book report by putting down the title of the book, the main characters in the book, and then a short synopsis of the story? Have you ever thought of other ways to report on a book? Is it possible to report on a book other than by writing about the book? Today we will attempt to determine other ways for book reports.

For the next few minutes we are going to "storm the brain" for ideas concerning how we might report on a book we have read. This experience will be fun for all of us if we follow four simple rules. (Put on board).

1. Criticism is ruled out.
2. "Freewheeling" is welcomed. (The wilder the idea the better.)

3. Quantity is desired.

4. Combination and improvement of ideas are sought.

(Appoint recorders from opposite sides of the room.)

I will knock on my desk when one of the rules seems violated. Just raise both hands when you desire to express a "hitchhike" idea.

Lesson Development:

What different ways may we make book reports? Suggested categories for book reporting (to be inserted as the flow of ideas diminishes):

1. *Drama:*
   A child could dramatize the book he read by using puppets as principal characters in the book and acting out an important incident in the book.

2. *Drawing:*
   A pupil could report this book by drawing comic strips to report the important sequences of the story in the book read.

3. *Machine reporting:*
   A child who had read the book could report dramatic scene by use of the tape recorder and present it to the class members.

4. *Discussion:*
   Several people who had read the same book could meet together and discuss the book with one another.

UTILIZING AFTERTHOUGHTS:

Now that it seems as if our group is "dry" of ideas, let us determine how many have been produced in the last fifteen minutes. (Ask the recorders to give the number and to suggest categories.) Do you suppose that we *could* produce even more ideas if we were really to try? That is just what I want you to do.

ASSIGNMENT:

Let us each write out our problem and the categories suggested by our recorders. Keep the problem in mind until tomorrow when I will call for your additional ideas. Just keep your mind open, jotting down ideas as they occur to you. Such afterthoughts may occur to you when least expected, so keep pencil and paper near you at all times.

PROCESSING IDEAS (second day):

(Take up lists of additional ideas and pass along to the recorders.)

I am appointing a committee of five to screen, edit, and categorize your ideas of how we can report on books read. (The teacher will assist the committee as needed.) We will each receive a reproduced list of this master list.

IMPLEMENTING IDEAS (third and fourth days):

Study our list of ideas and check two or three of these which you wish to use for reporting a book you have read.

ASSIGNMENT:

Your task is to report on a book you have read utilizing a suggested idea. Keep in mind that the idea may be expanded and altered as you apply your imagination. You should write out the original idea, however. We will then let the class try to relate your book report to our list of ideas.

DERIVING GENERALIZATIONS:

As a result of this experience a number of principles or ideas are evident, relative to book reporting. Let us list some of these:

SUGGESTIVE IDEAS (to be derived by pupils):
1. Book reports can be "fun."
2. Variety in book reports are interesting for everyone concerned.
3. We learn about drama and art when making book reports.

VALUES

Applied imagination, through brainstorming, may open doors to truly creative individual effort.

The ideation session tends to minimize existing inhibitions which ordinarily tend to block creativity.

Brainstorming is useful in piling up alternatives to the resolution of problems. Effective problem solving is necessarily limited by the possible solutions perceived by the individual(s) involved.

The brainstorming experience tends to generate enthusiasm for learning. By capturing the imagination, most pupils progress at an accelerated rate.

LIMITATIONS AND PROBLEMS

Despite the many values of group brainstorming, individual ideation usually
is more valuable and can be just as productive. Actually the process
incorporates both individual and group ideation in a three-stage approach: individual ideation, group brainstorming, and individual
ideation.

The effectiveness of a brainstorming session is dependent upon the appropriateness of the problem employed. There is a decided tendency
among teachers to select complex, as opposed to simple, problems.

Production of ideas through brainstorming is merely an initial phase of
creativity. Analytical problem-solving techniques must complement
production of ideas.

Brainstorming places the leader (teacher) in a new role. Instead of passing
judgment and suggesting direction, he must develop an atmosphere
of freedom from existing inhibitions. Some teachers (as well as
pupils) experience difficulty in making such a transition.

ILLUSTRATED BRAINSTORMING MEMOS

I. Useful in social studies area (first or second grade)

Concept: Safety rules of school prevent accidents.

Problem: How can we prevent accidents on the school grounds?

Suggested Categories:

1. Playground equipment
   Use styrofoam- and rubber-protected playground
   equipment.
2. Children
   Wear protective clothing.
3. Automation
   Have "people-movers" that keep children from fall-
   ing or running into others.

II. Useful in the science area (third or fourth grade)

Concept: Plants, properly displayed, will interest people to see
our work.

Problem: How can we display the plants we have grown for
open house?

Suggested Categories:
  1. Colored lights
       Colored lights to make the display pretty.
  2. Labeling
       Paper placed behind the plants to label the plant parts.
  3. Grouping
       Place the same kind of plants together in a separate display throughout the room.

III. Useful in the music area (upper grades)

Concept: Music portrays moods to the listener.

Problem: In what ways are moods reflected in music?

Suggested Categories:
  1. Loud
       Music that is loud may show excitement.
  2. Soft
       Music that is soft may show calmness.
  3. Rhythm
       Music rhythm may show action.
  4. Instruments used
       Various individual instruments are used to show various moods.

9

DISCUSSION METHODS

When individuals engage in discussion, they ponder or meditate; they think critically. The discussant *reflects* upon his ideas along with those of his peers. He is a searcher, an inquirer. In effect, he says, "Here are my ideas. How do they relate to your opinions and the facts of the situation?" He is willing to alter views which seem inadequate under the scrutiny of thoughtful analysis. He does not change his views, however, on the basis of peer pressure or emotion. If the objective evidence seems to warrant reassessments of tentative ideas and assumptions, he is ever ready to adjust accordingly.

Discussion is most appropriate when basic areas of controversy exist. Although a rather poor means of disseminating information, the method is ideal for evolving, sorting, and sifting facts and values essential for the resolution of problems. Discussion is ideally suited for attainment of the higher cognitive goals; it is useful also for attainment of affective goals.

FUNDAMENTAL PROPERTIES

Discussion essentially embodies the basic properties of the democratic process. It is based upon the assumption that individuals, when sufficiently informed on an issue, are capable of decision making in an atmosphere characterized by a free interchange of ideas and expressions.

Whether the leader is a teacher or a pupil, his role is essentially one of creating an appropriate environment for open reflection.

Open-mindedness

The discussant is receptive to new ideas. He examines or ponders new ideas alongside his own notions, making objective comparisons and contrasts. Above all, he must cultivate the ability to look at himself and his ideas objectively and dispassionately. First of all, he seeks to identify his own biases and prejudices. He must seek to avoid either-or thinking, recognizing the possibility of middle ground. This does not mean, of course, that he must change his attitudes. It does suggest, however, that each participant probably will see his own notions as not quite as good and the ideas of others as not quite as bad as he had originally seen them.

Flexibility

As implied in the foregoing, the discussant is willing to change his mind on the basis of logical, objective evidence. He does not necessarily do so, however. If, on the basis of his considered judgment, other ideas must be rejected, he stands his ground.

Even when discussion evolves into opposing camps, the discussant must be flexible enough to understand other views from the frame of reference of those involved. In rare instances a discussion group may merely agree to disagree.

Objectivity

Although the spirit and life of a discussion is projected through basic human emotion, intellectual processes of objectivity are emphasized. Ideas advanced by others are accepted on their own merits. Sources of information are frequently cited; evidence which might discredit certain facts or evaluations is brought into the open forum of reflection. Emotionalism, through persuasive language and gestures, is definitely discouraged. Even in a teacher-led discussion, contributions or inferences by the teacher must be open to careful scrutiny.

Reflective Processes

The basic purpose of discussion is to reflect upon information and ideas which lead to the resolution of a stated problem. Accordingly, there are no speeches in a discussion. One makes his point, contributes a bit of information or asks a question and then waits for somebody else to react to his contribution. The discussion leader (a pupil or teacher) reflects questions back to the group for analysis. Even in a teacher-led discussion the teacher must be viewed as one of a panel of equals. In attempting to accomplish this "impossible" task, he should restrict himself to skillful questions designed to encourage penetrating analysis and evaluation of ideas.

DISCUSSION PROCEDURE

When people associate with each other, they usually discuss. Individuals often find solutions to their daily problems by talking them over with others. Ask your neighbor what he thinks of the slate of candidates for the school board and he will probably respond with, "I don't know; what do you think?" After some *discussion* it is quite likely that both you and your neighbor will have clarified your views on the problem. Such informal discussion goes on continually in and out of the classroom. Indeed it is basic to the democratic process.

To be most effective as an instructional method, however, discussion must be carefully planned and executed. Although there are a number of variations and interesting modifications, the basic aims of discussion are to stimulate analysis, to encourage interpretations, and to develop or change attitudes. In this section a technique which embodies all these aims is described. Through appropriate leadership, evidence is brought to bear on the crucial aspects of a selected problem; the evidence is evaluated and analyzed by *the group*; certain proposed solutions are introduced and evaluated; and finally generalizations are derived from the experience.

Identifying the Problem

Discussion often breaks down because of the wording of the discussion problem. Four major types or kinds of questions have been identified. All may become involved during the discussion process. The *policy* question, however, is basic to the problem-solving type of discussion emphasized in this chapter. It should serve as a major problem for discussion. The four kinds of problems that lend themselves to varying degrees of reflective thinking are described below.

1. *Fact.* Problems of the fact are concerned with the discovery and evaluation of factual information. They are emphasized during the analysis of the problem when facts are introduced and clarified. For example: "What are the rules, if any, concerning making noise in the school hallway?"

2. *Value.* Problems of value are concerned with matters relative to value judgments. They call for the application of accepted standards in determining the appropriateness, rightness or effectiveness of an issue. For example: "How well are our school rules being followed?" Questions of value arise frequently during the early phases of a discussion. They are related to the *evaluation* of facts.

    Problems of fact and problems of value usually can be identified by the presence of some form of the verb *to be.* Indeed they are sometimes referred to as *is* or *are* questions.

3. *Advocacy.* As the term implies, problems of advocacy focus upon specific solutions. Such a question encourages argument rather than discussion. Advocacy questions most often emerge when hypotheses or tentative solutions to a problem are being evaluated. It is for this reason that establishment of accepted criteria should be developed prior to weighing the alternatives. To illustrate the type of question: "Should more school rules be added concerning noise in the school hallway?" The question can be answered by yes or no. Wording of the question precludes consideration of other alternatives. Such questions usually begin with the word "Should" or "Ought."

4. *Policy.* Problems of policy deal with matters necessitating decisions or action. Implied in the problem is the importance of exploring all possible solutions. Policy questions often begin with the words "What," "How," or "Why." The words "should" or "ought" are also stated or implied in the question. For example: "What should be the policy about making noise in the school hallway?"

In resolving a problem of policy, questions of *fact, value, and advocacy* will be involved. The reverse does not follow, however. In formulating problems for discussion, teachers often confuse policy with advocacy questions. Advocacy immediately directs attention to concern for one particular solution. Furthermore, it tends to divide a group into opposing camps.

Analyzing the Problem

As a preliminary step in decision making, the various components of a problem must be introduced and evaluated. The process leads the learner from definition of important terms to an inspection of important facts and circumstances associated with the problem. In this phase of discussion the seriousness of the problem is examined.

A discussion guide is offered for the problem, "What steps should be taken to get pupils to eat better foods?"

1. What foods are nutritious?
2. How common are poor diets among pupils?
3. What are the effects of poor diets?
4. What evidence indicates the problem is likely to persist? Are there evidences to the contrary?

Establishing Hypotheses

After all the pertinent facts and values have been carefully examined, the learner is ready to offer possible solutions to the problem. The advantages and disadvantages of each proposal are fully explored. While some of the alternatives will be suggested in various background reading references, pupils are encouraged to offer ideas of their own. Such ideas often are prompted during the analysis phase of the discussion. In this way, creative thinking is encouraged. To illustrate:

1. Television should advertise only nutritious foods.
2. It should be against the law to manufacture non-nutritious foods.

Deriving Generalizations

Sometimes the outcome of a problem-solving discussion is a definite plan of action. Thus by weighing each of the suggested hypotheses some decision relative to one or more preferred courses of action may emerge. In most classes, however, the scope of the problem will be too broad to achieve such an end.

Most class discussion experiences culminate with the derivation of generalizations which emerge from the experience.   To illustrate:

1. Poor diets can affect a person's health.
2. Nutritious foods help an individual to grow and develop properly.

Role of the Teacher as Discussion Leader

The appropriate use of questions is basic to effective class discussion.   Both student and teacher questions must be stated clearly and impartially.   It is relatively easy for a biased leader to influence the discussion process by interjecting slanted questions from time to time.   The question, "Why are non-nutritious foods dangerous?", for example, merely calls for support for a preconceived point of view.   A better question might be, "What are the effects of non-nutritious foods?"

An effective discussion leader must know how to handle nonrelated or remotely related questions.   In the spontaneous interplay of individual reactions to issues, a variety of questions tends to emerge.   The teacher must continually make quick decisions as to the desirability of pursuing given questions.   To push the group too forcibly can impede or even block group reflection, while to entertain any and all questions can lead to a myriad of blind alleys, resulting in little or no progress.   Sometimes the wise leader-teacher simply may ask the questioner, "Would you tell us how that is related to our problem?"   Some teachers practice putting both the problem and key questions on the board *in advance* of the discussion; this practice tends to keep the issue constantly before the group.

In class discussion, pupil questions usually are redirected to the group. It can be assumed that the teacher has a fairly good understanding of the discussion problem when the discussion begins.   His purpose, then, is to provide an opportunity for the group to develop an understanding by discussing the problem through to a conclusion.   The act of answering questions tends to emphasize his role as an "expert."   Few individuals do their best thinking when they are constantly reminded that the leader already "knows" the answers.   Under such conditions they are inclined merely to let this person think for them.   Redirection of pupil questions tends to bring out new relationships and interpretations.   If a question is vague, the redirecting of it to the child doing the asking is sometimes appropriate.   A rephrasing of a question will be in order at other times.

Skillful teachers generally adopt an air of acceptance when dealing with pupil responses to questions. If, however, a response obviously is in error, pupils themselves can handle the situation if adequate time for reflection is provided. Inaccurate responses may stimulate further questions and analysis designed to evoke reappraisal of the issue. Undue pupil embarrassment should be carefully avoided, however, if reflection is to continue. A teacher sometimes accepts an inaccurate response temporarily, simply by calling for other ideas pertaining to the issue. Usually subsequent responses will clarify the inaccuracy. (Occasionally the matter may have to be clarified before the group is permitted to advance to the next point.)

Reflection demands time! The glib person can impede such thinking. The teacher-leader inadvertently can encourage glibness by rushing responses unnecessarily. The pressure of time frequently contributes to this problem. As one pupil expressed it, "He doesn't care what you say so long as you say it in a hurry." There are times, however, when through a sudden insight an individual needs to make a quick response. This is usually evidenced by the unusual eagerness of the respondent.

PANEL PROCEDURE

Panel discussion involves a group of five to eight pupils who are seeking agreement on a problem of concern to themselves and to the children in the classroom. Like class discussion, it is structured around a problem of policy. Occasionally a panel may be formed for the purpose of exploring problems of fact if the evidence is highly controversial and/or contradictory. Such an *enlightenment* discussion, however, must be followed with an appropriate policy problem if the higher cognitive goals are to be achieved. Panel discussion contains many of the elements of freedom characteristic of democratic decision making. The threat of manipulation toward predetermined ends is minimized in panel discussion.

Identifying the Problem

Sometimes appropriate problems for panel discussion evolve from ongoing classroom activity. By recognizing the inadequacies of existing policy, for example, pupils may express a desire to explore other ways of resolving a difficulty. For example, one group of children which was studying conservation wondered if the policy should be changed so no one could hunt wild animals, like deer. For the discussion, the teacher assisted the group in formulating the problem: "What steps should be taken to change the policy concerning hunting?"

Frequently, panel discussion is anticipated and preplanned by the teacher. It is a relatively simple matter to identify those areas of greatest controversy within a given unit. It is essential, however, that pupils fully recognize such areas themselves before panel groups are established. They must accept the problem as their own if enthusiasm is to be assured.

After a problem area has been identified, the teacher must assist the panel group to formulate the problem into one of policy. If left to their own resources, pupils are likely to suggest a definite proposal. For example, "Should hunters be allowed to hunt wild animals?" Although such a discussion may be fruitful, the problem tends to eliminate other worthwhile proposals that warrant consideration. Furthermore, it tends to divide a discussion group into opposing camps. Such an attitude is not conducive to the open-mindedness normally associated with discussion.

Selecting and Organizing the Panel

The panel group is selected on the basis of expressed interest. A ten to fifteen minute initial planning session is necessary for the selection of a panel leader and division of labor if the problem is a complex one. The most enthusiastic, able, and tolerant pupil should be selected leader. Some groups may need help from the teacher with this task. The problem is then subdivided into subtopics for individual research if the problem is complex. (The leader will study all subtopics so that he may acquire a much needed over-all view of the problem.) For example, the problem "What steps should be taken to change the policy concerning hunting?" might be subdivided as follows:

1. Hunting policies
2. Overpopulation of animals
3. Wildlife refuges
4. Animal sanctuaries

Under optimum conditions each person is equally qualified in all aspects of the problem. However, time limitations and complexities of many problems, often render some division of labor desirable. Each member should have at least a workable knowledge of all aspects of the problem. Such background information can be attained from assigned textbook readings.

For most panel problems pupils will need a short time to prepare for the presentation; older elementary pupils may need about a week for preparation time. The teacher will work closely with the discussion leader. For larger problems some teachers have followed the practice of asking the chairman for a brief progress report each day to insure continued progress. After the group has completed its investigation of the problem, it should meet briefly to discuss the major aspects of the problem to be explored. The discussion should not be rehearsed, however. Many teachers limit such discussion to a period of fifteen minutes. Formulation of specific questions should be avoided.

Responsibilities of Panel Members

The panel leader provides a liaison between the teacher and the other panelists. He guides and directs pupils in their background reading efforts. In preparation for the discussion experience, he prepares a list of guide questions. The teacher may have to help in the preparation of this list. The guide questions will remind him of the scope and sequence of the problem. They also provide a handy reference when discussion drags or bogs down. Most of his prepared questions will be posed by different panelists as they introduce and probe various issues. The discussion guide will be very similar to the key questions posed in the illustrated plan for class discussion.

Responsibilities of the Audience

Although the panelists discuss the problem among themselves, the experience is designed for the benefit of other class members also. Contributions must be audible to all. As discussion proceeds, the other class members are expected to participate vicariously in the reflective process. With older pupils, questions and points which need further clarification may be jotted down for use during the question period which follows the presentation. All children will want to participate in the question period following one panel discussion.

Responsibilities of the Teacher

The teacher must see that all members of the class follow the presentation fully. By establishing a few signals with the leader, he can encourage members to raise their voices, provide guidance for moving from one part of the discussion to another, and the like. Usually he will want to guide the learner in bringing the discussion to a close. A question period of from five to ten minutes is essential.

Leading the Follow-Through Discussion

Following the brief question period, the teacher leads the group in a follow-through discussion. This should follow the panel presentation. At this point pupils are expected to derive key generalizations from the experience; most of the generalizations should come from the members of the audience. Clarification and expansion of basic points are often needed. Thus the panelists become useful resource personnel. The teacher may also want to expand or introduce neglected points.

Preparation for the follow-through discussion is facilitated when the teacher jots down key points during the panel discussion for later reference. (He should also identify the pupil who makes each point.) In essence this becomes a useful guide for the follow-through experience.

It is desirable to take a look at the panel experience if other groups are to follow. Could all members be heard? Was there enough probing? Was proper balance achieved? This evaluation of the panel will help members of the class develop better participation in subsequent panels.

PLANNING FOR DISCUSSION

Discussion often breaks down as a result of inadequate pre-planning by the teacher. Although pupils themselves often suggest the need for a class discussion by the questions they ask, the teacher assumes responsibility for formulating the problem for discussion. Furthermore, he must develop a structured discussion guide which incorporates the essential dimensions of the discussion process. The lesson plan illustrated below is suggestive only.

LESSON PLAN ILLUSTRATION (health area—fifth or sixth grade)

Concept: Poor diets may affect an individual's health.

Problem: What steps should be taken to get pupils to eat better foods?

Goals: After the lesson the pupil should have furthered his understanding of the effects of poor diets on an individual, as evidenced by:

1. His contributions during the discussion process.
2. His ability to draw generalizations from the experience.

Lesson Approach:

Show a ten minute film, *Foods For Better Living.* Ask pupils to jot down questions immediately following the film presentation.

Lesson Development:

A. Analysis of the problem:
   1. What foods are nutritious?
   2. How common are poor diets among pupils?
   3. What are the effects of poor diets?
   4. Is the problem likely to continue? Why or why not?

B. Weighing alternatives:

   Now in view of our analysis of this problem, what steps should be taken to get pupils to eat better foods? The following are some types of solutions which may be offered:

   1. Organize an educational program designed to inform all pupils concerning nutritious foods.
   2. Pass laws against the manufacture of non-nutritious foods. (Advantages and disadvantages of each proposal will be treated fully.)

Deriving Generalizations:

From our discussion, what important generalizations seem apparent? Examples of points which may be advanced are as follows:

1. Poor diets can affect a person's health.
2. Nutritious foods help an individual to grow and develop properly.

VALUES

Group discussion involves the processes of give and take essential to a democratic system.

Prejudices and biases are frequently modified when subjected to the scrutiny of the peer group.

The combined critical thinking of a group is much more likely to correct deficiencies in evidence and reasoning than an individual might.

The processes of discussion involve cooperation and group sharing of ideas. Thus judgments tend to improve.

The technique tends to render the student progressively less dependent upon the teacher.

LIMITATIONS AND PROBLEMS

Discussion presupposes adequate preparation. It is impossible to reflect effectively upon facts and concepts which are unknown or incompletely understood.

The permissive characteristic of discussion tends to encourage digression.

The discussion leader may be unable to maintain an open mind.

Even when carefully organized, class discussion is unpredictable.

Group agreement or consensus does not insure accomplishment.

ILLUSTRATED DISCUSSION OUTLINES

    I.   Useful in the science area (primary grades)

        Unit: Weather

        Concept: Cloud types indicate weather changes.

        Problem: How can clouds help us to know what the weather will be like?

        Sample Analysis Questions:

           1. What does a cirrus cloud tell us?

           2. What does a cumulus cloud tell us about the weather?

           3. What do stratus clouds indicate?

    II. Useful in the language arts area (fourth, fifth or sixth grades)

        Unit: Written communication

        Concept: Writing autobiographies enable a child to be observant of the things that go on around him.

Problem: What is the best way to author a story of one's personal experiences?

Sample Analysis Questions:

   1. What made the autobiography, *Ben and Me*, interesting?
   2. What makes autobiographies different from other stories?
   3. What kinds of events take place in autobiographies?
   4. What words make the autobiography more real?

Some Possible Solutions to Consider:

   1. The things that happen are everyday events.
   2. The autobiography tells the story of a person.
   3. The autobiography is about yourself.
   4. Words such as "I" or "we" make the story more real.

III. Useful in the health area (seventh or eighth grade)

   Unit: Microorganisms

   Concept: Respiratory diseases are transmitted in many ways.

   Problem: How can the transmission of respiratory diseases be minimized?

   Sample Analysis Questions:

      1. What are some common respiratory diseases?
      2. What are airborne microorganisms?
      3. How are they transmitted?
      4. Why is the problem more important today than in the past?

   Some Possible Solutions to Consider:

      1. Pass strict laws on air pollution.
      2. Require inoculations against disease.
      3. Require medical checkups.
      4. Require regular chest X-rays.

IV. Useful in social studies area (fourth or fifth grade)

   Unit: Pioneers

   Concept: Pioneers were motivated to move West for various reasons.

   Problem: What reasons did the pioneers have for moving West?

   Sample Analysis Questions:

      1. What was happening to the fertile lands in the eastern part of the United States?
      2. Why did Mark Twain and people like him move West?

3. Why did miners and prospectors go to the western part of the United States?
4. Where were the population centers in the United States?
5. What freedoms were enjoyed by the pioneers who moved West?

Sample Possible Solutions to Consider:

1. Many pioneers moved West for new lands.
2. Some pioneers moved to the western part of the United States for adventure.
3. Gold enticed many pioneers to go West.
4. Many moved West because they felt the cities were too crowded.
5. Some moved West to escape jail sentences and to make a new life.

10

THE DRAMATIC PLAY METHOD

In dramatic play, role playing is used as a vehicle to portray a situation for study and analysis. It involves the spontaneous enactment of a realistic life problem in the realm of interpersonal relationships. When used effectively it may enable the learner to improve his response to a situation, to increase his repertoire of responses, and to increase his sensitivity to the feelings of others.

FUNDAMENTAL PROPERTIES

Any meaningful portrayal of a selected life experience depends upon its immediacy and relevancy to the lives of those involved. Almost any concept can be related to problems of everyday living so long as the learner is able to project himself into the situation. The properties which follow are essential to a realistic setting.

Determining Pupil Readiness

When the learner recognizes inadequacies of previous behaviors, he is challenged to seek new ways of coping with situations. Various techniques can be used to create an awareness of inadequate understanding of a concept. For example, the following concept may be involved: Empathic ability aids in the resolution of different points of view. To test readiness or to determine the present level of understanding, the learner may be shown a film and asked to cite evidence of empathy or lack of it and to identify factors that appeared to block the empathic process. Other techniques might include an analysis of a story, written examples from past experience or an open-ended problem situation. The learner may be asked to indicate how he would react to a problem situation and then to designate those behaviors which show empathic ability. Such experiences help the learner realize his need for expanding his understanding of the concept and for improving his skill in applying appropriate principles in the area.

Affective Considerations

Problems of interaction usually are associated with man's inability to understand the impact of human emotions. Thus a dramatized situation can be structured around a conflict situation, the resolution of which demands some insight into the basic needs of the other person. The objective is to determine the impact of specific events upon feeling reactions of those involved.

Realistic Situation

A situation close to the lives of the pupils is a basic essential of the dramatic play experience. Unlike drama, which often re-creates scenes far removed from pupil experiences, a dramatic play situation is developed from the everyday lives of those involved. For example, one does not play a role of George Washington, or the Queen of England or even of some local adult figure. A youngster plays roles which are within the realm of his personal experience. He does not play an identifiable life role which may, in effect, subject his own inadequacies to public display. A black does not play the role of a black, nor does a poor, generally unkempt individual play the role of such an individual.

Simplicity

Although human interaction varies from the simple to the complex, analysis is greatly facilitated when the situation is kept as simple as possible. Situations involving two pupils are preferred. Additional players not only complicate the analysis but also may place one member of the cast on the defensive unnecessarily. There seems to be a tendency to "gang up" on the underdog. Sometimes additional players may be added if the situation is replayed.

Spontaneity

The situation for enactment is not rehearsed. Indeed, the participants are selected immediately after the situation has been developed. After one has been projected into his role, the way it is played is not a critical issue. The individual is instructed to react to the situation as he feels at the time. If certain comments or inferences have a positive reaction, for example, he will reflect this through his own behavior just as any individual might behave. Likewise, feelings of indifference or even negative reactions are reflected through various behaviors. One makes no effort to telescope such feelings, however. They are allowed to develop in as natural a manner as possible.

DRAMATIC PLAY PROCEDURE

Dramatic play should be viewed as a series of steps with each step necessary to a successful learning experience. Inasmuch as the method focuses upon human emotions, careful planning is essential if a sound psychological climate is to be maintained.

Problem Identification

From his identified concept, the teacher formulates a problem to be solved. After pupils are made aware of their present inadequacies in the area, the problem is placed on the board for all to see. From the concept, "Empathic ability aids in the resolution of different points of view," the following problem might be evolved: "How can we further appreciate another person's point of view?" In this manner, pupils are made aware of the concept to be learned in language that they can understand.

Defining the Situation and Roles

The specific situation for enactment is based upon the felt needs of the learner. For example, the teacher may ask, "What instances can you recall from your own lives which illustrate lack of empathy?" He then suggests that one of these be acted out through a skit. The broad situation may be developed by pupils (with teacher guidance), or it may be preplanned by the teacher. If the broad situation is preplanned by the teacher, pupils should assist in developing details of the situation.

To illustrate, using the problem of empathy: someone (or the teacher) may suggest a situation where a new child has moved into the neighborhood school. The broad situation is then placed upon the board.

Susie, a fourth grader, has moved into a new school.
Her father is in the service.
She moves quite frequently.
Susie needs to make new friends.

At this point, pupils fill in some details of the situation, such as Susie's problems of getting acquainted with new children, Susie's characteristics, and possibly some characteristics of Ruth who lives near Susie.

After assuring the group that one's acting ability is not to be evaluated, a volunteer cast is selected. Susie (the one who is to lead the conversation) is then asked to leave the room while the class adds additional points relative to the situation as seen by Ruth who lives near Susie. These would be factors and feelings which would definitely influence the situation but which would not be fully appreciated nor understood by Susie. For example: Ruth has not gone out of her way to meet Susie. Susie may not want to get acquainted with Ruth. Ruth has her other friends.

Preparing the Class for Observation and Analysis

The class is asked to watch for clues which are indicative of the situation as it develops. What questions or comments seem to contribute to or detract from the development of empathy? What clues are (or are not) pursued? What behaviors indicate that Susie (or Ruth) did or did not understand each other's feelings? Why did you identify with either Susie or Ruth? How else might the situation be handled to show empathy?

Dramatic Play

Prior to the return of the leading character, the teacher assists the other players in identifying their roles. He may briefly summarize the situation or he may ask two or three leading questions, for example, "What do you think of Susie?" "What plans do you have to help Susie feel welcome?"

Susie is called into the room. The teacher then prepares Susie for the role she is to play. How old are you? How long have you lived in this town? How will you make new friends?

The players are instructed to react to their role situations just as the events make them feel. The dramatic play continues uninterrupted for about five or ten minutes. Action is cut when enough of the scene has been portrayed to enable the audience to analyze the situation.

Analyzing the Situation

When the drama is stopped, the teacher will want to ask three or four key questions designed to draw attention to the situation. The following are suggested:

1. Might this situation actually have occurred? (A "yes" answer is expected.)
2. (To those reacting to the situation) How did you feel as the situation developed?
3. (To the leader of the situation) Did you feel as if you were making progress?
4. (To the class) What clues did we get which may account for these feelings?

The class then recalls comments and nonverbal expressions which reflected changes in feeling reactions. The players are used as resources to substantiate various forms of the analysis. Attention is continually directed to the processes of interaction; criticism of how the roles were played is forbidden.

Finally, after the enacted situation has been thoroughly analyzed some attention is directed toward other approaches which might have been employed. Sometimes it is desirable to replay the situation.

Related Situations

Following the analysis, pupils must be made aware of the variety of similar situations which could have been selected for analysis. Thus they recognize the generalizability of the concept. Empathic ability, for example, is needed in a wide variety of interaction situations. These include other children groups, older groups, and contacts with younger children.

Deriving Generalizations

As a culminating activity, pupils are asked to formulate generalizations from the experience. Generalizations should apply equally well to any number of related situations. Pupils may be asked to perform this task individually by writing them out, or they may do it jointly through class discussions and make an experience chart. In any event, generalizations represent the basic learnings which result from the dramatic play experience.

To illustrate:

1. A feeling for another person is increased when you put yourself in his place.
2. Friendship may be developed when one is willing to be a friend.
3. Words, phrases or body movements sometimes reveal hidden feelings.

PLANNING FOR DRAMATIC PLAY

The illustrated plan is designed to clarify further the essential steps of employing the dramatic play method of teaching. Although each teacher eventually will develop his own techniques in the area, none of the steps included in the "Lesson Development" can be safely omitted.

LESSON PLAN ILLUSTRATION (health area)

Concept: Empathic ability aids in assisting someone to get acquainted in an unfamiliar place.

Problem: How can we help a child who moves into our school?

Goals: After this lesson the pupil should have increased his sensitivity to the feelings of others, as evidenced by:

1. His ability to detect clues to hidden feelings.
2. His ability to identify specific ways to help a person get acquainted in a new setting.
3. His ability to derive valid generalizations as a result of the experience.

Lesson Approach:

In our health class it mentioned the problem people have when they move to new places. Because we have a lot of new pupils moving in and out of our classroom, perhaps we can take this as our problem situation, act it out, and then analyze it in relation to our feelings for others. (Pupil) Let's take a situation in which a girl moves into our class. (Other pupils give approval.) Fine. We will develop the situation that follows.

Lesson Development:

A. Broad situation:

1. Susie, a fourth grader, has moved into a new school.
2. Her father is in the service.
3. She moves quite frequently.
4. Susie needs to make new friends.

B. Details of the situation: (Class develops.) Concentrate on general aspects of Susie and Ruth who lives near Susie.

C. Threat reduction: In this type of experience no one is to be criticized on his acting ability. There is no right or wrong way of doing this.

D. Selection of players: Volunteers (One should not be permitted to play his real-life role.)

E. Send leading character from the room.

F. Fill in additional details: (by class)

1. How may Susie feel in the new school?
2. Why does Ruth want to know Susie?
3. What about Ruth's other friends?

G. Preparation of class for observation and analysis:

1. Remember to jot down key words and phrases that seem to affect feelings—either positively or negatively.
2. Note expressions on pupils' faces.

H. Warm up the players:
   1. Who are you?
   2. What time of day is it?
I. Play (No more than ten minutes).
J. Analysis of the situation:
   1. How did the play come out?
   2. How did you feel? (To each of the players in turn)
   3. What clues did we get which may have accounted for these feelings?
K. Related situations: What similar situations can you recall which illustrated this feeling or a lack of it?

Deriving Generalizations:

What generalizations can we draw from this experience which might also apply to many other related situations? For example:

1. A feeling for another person is increased when you put yourself in his place.
2. Friendship may be developed when one is willing to be a friend.

VALUES

Dramatic play provides the learner with new insights into possible responses to social situations.

The method increases one's sensitivity to the feelings of others in conflict situations.

Through dramatic play, an individual is able to project himself into the shoes of another. Realism is maintained without the usual threat to one's personality which characterizes analysis of actual life situations.

The enactment of selected situations provides a rare opportunity for discussion of actual feeling reactions.

LIMITATIONS AND PROBLEMS

The dramatic play experience demands meticulous planning of a series of steps. A breakdown at any point may block the learner's ability to portray a realistic situation.

The problem must be of immediate concern to those involved. In some subject areas realistic parallels are difficult to visualize.

Discussion analysis must focus on the situation at all times. When rapport in the situation is not effectively established, there may be a tendency to criticize the players.

As employed in the dramatic play experience, role playing is merely a tool for developing understanding. Therapy—emphasizing the motives behind the roles played—has no place in the classroom. The tendency of some teachers to select a role for the purpose of "putting somebody in his place" should be avoided.

ILLUSTRATED DRAMATIC PLAY SITUATIONS

I.   Useful in language arts area (fourth through sixth grades)
   Unit: Telephone Courtesy
   Concept: Courtesy in answering the telephone is appreciated
   Broad Situation:
   1. People call on the telephone. John shouts "Hello."
   2. John keeps his lips too close to the telephone.
   3. People dislike calling because John is rude to them on the telephone.

II.   Useful in the reading area (primary grades)
   Unit: Oral Reading
   Concept: Consideration of others who are reading orally
   Broad Situation:
   1. Billy is a poor oral reader.
   2. He hates to read because others laugh at him.
   3. Billy is self-conscious when he reads his experience stories to class members.

III.   Useful in the social studies area (kindergarten, first or second grades)
   Unit: Work in the Home
   Concept: Everyone in the family must share in the work.
   Broad Situation:
   1. Mary does not pick up her clothes or put away her toys.
   2. Mary's parents scold her for not doing her share of the work in the home.

3. Mary screams and cries when she is told to pick up her clothes
4. Mary throws her toys around the house.

IV. Useful in spelling and handwriting areas (first through sixth grades)

Unit: Written Communication

Concept: Must spell and write in an acceptable manner for written communication to take place.

Broad Situation:

1. Frank does not feel he needs to practice handwriting or spell words properly.
2. Frank dislikes it when his teacher corrects his handwriting and spelling.
3. Children in Frank's class cannot read his reports or stories.

V. Useful in the science area (upper grades)

Unit: Procedures for Science Experiments

Concept: Responsibility is necessary to eliminate accidents.

Broad Situation:

1. Kenneth and Jane were "goofing around" during their science experiment.
2. Their teacher told them that accidents can occur when pupils are not careful with scientific experiments and equipment.
3. Kenneth and Jane felt their teacher was unreasonable concerning the rules.

11

SIMULATION GAME METHOD

Any number of complex social problems confront the pupils in this nation today. Usually such problems possess many variables which bear upon appropriate solutions. Most instructional methods are designed to approach a given problem from a single framework of decision making. Nevertheless, it is recognized that a wholly appropriate solution might be rendered wholly *inappropriate* when other parties or frames of reference are considered. This has led to the development of the simulation method which is currently creating considerable attention among elementary school-teachers everywhere.

FUNDAMENTAL PROPERTIES

A *simulation* is an artificial, condensed representation of reality. It may reproduce the essential details of either a model or an actual situation. Governing the conduct of a simulation are rules which limit or proscribe the actions of players. Rules are incorporated into a *game* of some type for the purpose of introducing the elements of competition, cooperation, and conflict as they normally occur in real life.[1]

[1] Dale M. Garvey, *Simulation, Role-Playing and Sociodrama* (The Emporia State Research Studies, 16, no. 2, Emporia, Kansas, 1967), p. 11.

Game Rules

Rules of a simulation game perform three distinct functions.

1. They specify the distribution of resources among the players as the game begins.
2. They state relationships among the various elements of the game, including players, resources, moves, and winning or losing.
3. They describe the mode of sequence of play.

Role Playing and Dramatic Play

Simulation incorporates both role playing and dramatic play in addition to a third element—a game.[2] Instead of seeking solutions to a single problem, several interacting problems are involved. Like dramatic play, simulation is based upon some element of social conflict. Solution(s) must be acceptable to the majority of the members of the group represented. Unlike dramatic play, the game is the element which determines the winner or loser.

Representation of Reality

A simulation *model* is a simplified representation of reality, reduced to manageable proportions. It attempts to include those elements of reality which are essential to the processes under investigation. Simulations or operating models have been in use for some time.

Resource Materials

Currently simulation games are being enthusiastically developed and used by teachers. Commercially developed games are available which depict historical events, economic development, consumer behavior, and city life. There are games of world trade, games involving principles of developing nations, buying, the money system, and life in a society living near the survival level. Many teachers (and pupils) are developing their own simulation games.

---

[2] In the context of this chapter the terms "simulations" and "simulation games" are synonymous.

SIMULATION GAME PROCEDURES

Too often the design and use of simulation games are left to hit-or-miss procedures. Many people are currently writing about their experiences in general terms, but few have bothered to suggest the specific steps followed. Like dramatic play (and indeed most methods of teaching), the simulation game is another approach to problem solving. Unlike other methods, however, this involves a complex situation necessitating *resolution of several problems* as the situation develops. The steps identified in this section should greatly facilitate the appropriate application of the method.

Identifying the Problem

A simulation game embodies at least two or three closely related unit concepts. Basic to the development of a simulation game is conflict or the clash of opposing forces or desires. As with any other method, concepts provide the basis for development of goals and anticipated behavioral outcomes. For example, behaviors which would suggest added tolerance and respect for those who hold opposing or differing social attitudes might be identified.

Developing the Model

Using the identified basic concepts as a guide, the teacher must develop a rough outline of the game to be portrayed. It may be hypothetical or a replication of an actual process. In any event, it must be a selective representation of those elements necessary to achieve objectives. If too complex, pupils will become frustrated and may lose sight of the purposes entirely. If overly simple, the game may have little motivational value and may result in basic misconceptions concerning the complexities of actual events.

Above all, the teacher himself must explore in depth the essential elements to be utilized in the simulation. In evaluating the potential value of the proposed simulation, one might ask: "Do the elements to be portrayed look like the real thing?" The simulation need not look like the real thing in all respects but only those that are relevant to the study at hand.

Creating the rudimentary outline of a simulation game is the "giant step" of the process. It is at this point that creative imagination is essential. Once the broad aspects of the experience have been created, the details can be readily developed.

Identifying Teams

The identification of roles to be played can be inferred from the model to be portrayed. They are built around the basic concepts previously identified for the situation. Class size, of course, is a practical consideration which will influence role assignments. It has been found that subgroups of four to six children are ideally suited for such purposes.

Role assignment may be made on a purely random basis, pupil choice, child's ability or sociometrically. Perhaps a combination of all the foregoing should be considered, dependent upon the nature of the group and simulation involved.

Game Resources

The relationships of the elements in a simulation game are made realistic through resources (raw materials, money, votes, etc.) to exchange in competition with other players. Although a precise quantification of power is not always evident in real life, most educational simulations attempt to assess precise values of resources exchanged.

Basic to any simulation game is appropriate use of audio visual materials. Such media are most useful in creating the simulated environment. In a production line simulation game, for example, the raw materials are essential for the activity.

Identifying and Developing Sequences of the Play and Final Payoff

A game is played in well-defined cycles, each structured around a crisis. Pupils must know the precise goals to be achieved and fully understand the rules of procedure to be followed. Rules limit the range and define the legitimate actions of the players.

Action begins with a "crisis" of some kind. In the illustrated simulation the crisis is to demonstrate the efficiency of the production line as compared to the output of individual workers. The first phase of Cycle I involves planning for the production line groups and the individual worker groups. The second phase is carried out by actual assignment of duties for the production line groups and the completed task necessary for the individual worker groups.

The third phase usually involves group action of some kind. In effect, the strategy, planned and developed in the previous phases, is now put into action. In the illustrated model, this phase is called the actual work load for production.

The final phase focuses upon the work completed and the organizational advantages of the production line groups and the individual worker groups, which is a logical consequence of the work project.

Other cycles can be planned which logically follow Cycle I as the occasion demands. Some games may consist of one cycle; others may incorporate three or more such cycles. The nature of the phases within a cycle depends somewhat upon the nature of the game. Usually they will involve a sequence of planning, assignments, action, and consequences.

Post-Game Discussion

A thorough post-game discussion is potentially the most valuable aspect of simulation. Each participant, having made one or more important decisions during the game, has been rewarded with a certain number of points (e.g., money, products completed, votes). One way to begin the discussion is to ask the highest and the lowest scoring players to describe their activities. By contrasting, general principles begin to emerge.

Since a simulation game represents an *abstract* of reality, a comparison of the experience with the actual or parallel situation is essential. In the illustration, for example, rewards were based upon products actually completed. Since a simulation cannot include all aspects of reality, the experience must be analyzed thoroughly for distortions of reality.

Finally, pupils should be guided in a critical derivation of concepts or generalizations. The process of becoming thoroughly involved in a conflict situation may cause the learner to temporarily lose sight of basic purposes involved. Pupil concepts will not necessarily correspond with those identified by the teacher during preplanning but they should be similar to them.

PLANNING FOR SIMULATION GAMES

As with any other method, the use of simulation games demands careful planning. The experience may be completed in one period of time but may extend for four or five days or longer. Since considerable preparation and warm-up is essential, a sufficient amount of time should be allowed. The following plan is suggestive of the intricate relationship involved.

LESSON PLAN ILLUSTRATION (social studies area—second grade)

Concepts: 1. Assembly line production requires workers to cooperate with one another to achieve their goal.
2. More items are produced per worker in assembly line production than an individual worker making the product by himself.

Problem: Which method will produce more decorations, the assembly line groups or the individual worker groups?

Goals: After this lesson, the pupil should have furthered his understanding of assembly line production and individual worker production, as evidenced by:
1. His ability to work effectively in his group.
2. His ability to resolve the problem and follow through in making the decorations.
3. His ability to analyze the problem of decoration production between the two major groups.

Lesson Approach:

In our study of various workers in our community, we have seen that each group of workers has special functions to perform.

Today we will work two different ways to determine the production differences of assembly line workers as compared to individual workers making the same product.

Each of us will be given a job and certain rules to follow. The game involves definite steps to follow with a time limit. The "winner" will be that group which succeeds in making the most decorations which are made a specific way.

Lesson Development:

The teacher will inform the groups as to the "crisis" or problem to be solved. Background information from the textbooks and various trade books are used. (Charts may be enlarged and reproduced for clarity. Use of an overhead projector may be most useful in this connection.)

A. *Phase I:* The situation begins with a planning session for the assembly line groups and the individual worker groups. Six groups of five each will be designated. Three groups will be individual worker groups and three groups will be production-assembly line groups. In addition, two or three reporters will be designated. The strategy for production line groups will be to delineate the specific jobs for each worker to perform, thus leading to the completed decoration. The strategy for individual worker groups will be that each will make the entire decoration by himself.

B. *Phase II:* The assembly-production line groups will make specific assignments to children for the tasks to be performed. Each child will perform one task on each decoration. The individual worker groups also will become familiar with the steps each one must follow to complete the decoration.

C. *Phase III:* Groups will assemble to make the decorations. All materials, scissors, paste, etc. will be available for each group. The work will continue until a specific amount of time has elapsed.

D. *Phase IV:* The groups will reflect upon the advantages of the assembly line production and the individual worker production.

(Length of each phase will vary, depending upon size and maturity of the group. The illustrated problem might consume additional time if additional cycles are introduced.)

Post-Game Discussion:

What groups have the least and most completed decoration? Would you describe your activities? For example:
1. What happened in the assembly-line worker groups?
2. What happened in the individual worker groups?
3. Why do we have assembly line workers in our community?
4. Why do we have individual workers in our community?

VALUES

Simulation games involve the pupil in an active, realistic problem-solving process. Simulation presents life-like problems or situations which challenge the participants to develop appropriate response.

The simulation game method leads pupils to the development of conceptual learnings.

Simulation offers a procedure for bridging the gap between theory and practice.

Participants consider the simulation experiences stimulating and highly motivating.

LIMITATIONS AND PROBLEMS

Even though the simulation game is life-like, not *all* factors can be simulated. By limiting the variables, simulation may lead to improper conclusions.

The time factor is important for simulation games. Teachers sometimes underestimate the number of hours needed for successful simulation games.

Choosing games beyond the child's maturity or qualifications will lead to frustration for the child and teacher.

Preparation for the simulation activity is essential. The teacher must prepare the children thoroughly and the teacher must understand the theoretical bases for the problem.

During the simulation game activity, children may become highly competitive and tempers may erupt. The teacher is cautioned to aid the child who develops these difficulties.

ILLUSTRATED SIMULATION GAME SITUATIONS

I. Useful in social studies area (fourth or fifth grade)

Unit: Geographical Features and the Growth of Cities

Concepts:

1. Geographical features help or hinder the growth of a city.
2. Industrial forces and competition for workers affect the growth of cities.
3. Planning and cooperation by city leaders and citizens affect the growth of cities.

Problem: What geographical features and forces work together in the development of large cities?

Goals: After this lesson, the pupil should have furthered his understanding of geographic features and forces which help in developing cities by:

1. His ability to work effectively in committees.
2. His ability to resolve a "crisis" problem of competing forces between cities in the development of a city.
3. His ability to critically analyze geographical features and determine how these features may hinder or help in the growth of a city.

II. Useful in the arithmetic area (fifth or sixth grade)

Unit: Fractions in Daily Life

Concepts:

1. Fractions are a useful part of the child's daily life.
2. Whole numbers and fractions written together are mixed numbers.
3. Mixed numbers are used in the stock market quotations in the local newspaper.
4. Prices of stock fluctuate from day to day.

Problem: Which group can choose the shares of stock that go up the most on the stock market?

Goals: After this lesson, the pupil should have furthered his understanding of mixed numbers as a useful part of daily living by:

1. His ability to work effectively in his group.
2. His ability to resolve the problem and figure price fluctuations of his group's selected stock.
3. His ability to determine the stock fluctuation among the groups within his class.
4. His ability to make trades with other groups and pick the best stock.

III. Useful in the social studies area (upper grades)

Unit: Inflation of a Money System

Concepts:

1. Supply of money influences prices.
2. Supply of materials to buy influences prices.

Problem: Which group could make the most finished products in the shortest period of time?

Goals: After this lesson, the pupil should have furthered his understanding of inflation of money by:

1. His bartering ability for needed materials to finish certain product assignments.
2. His ability to trade gold certificates when these certificates were scarce and plentiful for needed materials.
3. His ability to analyze the relationship between supply of money and supply of materials as they influenced prices.

12

TEACHER-PUPIL PLANNING TECHNIQUES

The art of living and working together harmoniously is the ultimate task of all mankind. That man has, thus far, failed miserably in achieving this goal is evident on all sides. From the highest levels of international relations to the man on the street, one sees evidences of man's inability to work cooperatively with his fellows.

Traditionally, the role of the teacher has been conceived as that of a taskmaster. Pupils have been expected to conform, to know *about* subject matter, to compete with one another for grades which, all too often, have become the ends of education. The situation still exists in many of the elementary school classrooms—*not* because the instructional approach is considered sound, but frequently because those involved simply are unable to break from years of conditioning when they themselves were students.

Democratic instructional procedures are probably best characterized through joint teacher-pupil planning. This procedure involves teacher and pupils working together cooperatively. It is one of freedom, of creativity, of self-direction. With teacher guidance, critical thinking is developed as pupils themselves set up their own problems for exploration and analysis. Thus tasks become self-imposed; activities become self-directed; evaluation becomes self-competitive.

FUNDAMENTAL PROPERTIES

The cooperative experience, like most other instructional approaches, involves the processes of inquiry. Unlike some other approaches, however, this technique is based upon current pupil needs and interests rather than upon organized bodies of subject matter as a starting point. Indeed, the processes of reflective thought are applied by the entire group. The topics which follow represent essential conditions necessary for effective application of the method.

Democratic Framework

Cooperative teacher-pupil planned experiences are conceived within a framework which may be new to both child and teacher. Teacher-imposed activities and assignments are replaced by problems and projects suggested by pupils themselves. A competitive class climate is replaced with a climate of cooperative group interaction as children pursue different aspects of a complex problem. All legitimate areas of choice must be identified and then resolved by the class group. The teacher's role is relegated to that of a participating guide. His task is that of guiding pupils in their objective consideration of issues: sometimes by acting as a resource person, by discouraging or even rejecting suggested actions which would carry children beyond the particular problem under investigation, or by offering suggestions and advice of his own. The basic objective is that of supplying guidance, assistance, and support at every step of the way *without* unnecessarily imposing his wishes or authority upon the group.

Immediate Applications

In selecting an appropriate topic for cooperative teacher-pupil involvement, attention must be directed to the immediate concerns of children. Some areas of school work are more directly related to the group than are others. There are areas within almost all subject areas in which immediate parallels can be found. If such parallels can be made apparent to pupils, *prior to a thorough investigation of the topic*, a teacher-pupil planned experience may be effective.

Flexibility

Children feel real concerns in many areas of their daily existence. If the teacher-pupil planned experience successfully touches their lives, the quantity and quality of questions will be almost overwhelming. Textbook units no longer will seem adequate, as questions tend to cut across topical areas. Some questions may seem more directly related to certain curriculum areas than the one under consideration. The answers to other questions will be difficult to find. A few questions may be embarrassing or even appear to go beyond the realm of prudence acceptable to school authorities.

Both teacher and pupils must be flexible in such matters. The teacher must be willing to revise his thinking with respect to units, recognizing that conventional lines often are extremely arbitrary. Questions which seem inappropriate for class consideration can be reworded to incorporate the basic idea in a more acceptable form. Sometimes a teacher will find it necessary to exclude questions which may be treated more appropriately in a different context or which are remotely related to the area. An explanation of such matters is desirable.

Resource Materials

The diversity of questions will render textbooks inadequate. One must search through library books, magazines, encyclopedias, yearbooks, and the like. Frequently, personal interviews with individuals knowledgeable in the area are appropriate; sometimes school trips and individual experimentation are needed. The teacher, anticipating such needs, must make preliminary arrangements for study groups in a variety of settings. Key books must be placed in the room; potential resource people must be contacted. Since pupils will be working somewhat independently of the teacher, expected rules of conduct must be clearly established.

Time Requirements

The processes of planning, researching, and reporting take time. Developing questions, establishing study groups, and researching a given area necessitates a time span of at least a week. Reporting, review, and evaluational activities will likely involve another week. On the other hand, most teachers have found that children vary greatly in their interest in a given problem area. The maturity of the children and their sustained interest in the problem must determine the time requirements.

TEACHER-PUPIL PLANNING PROCEDURES

The processes of teacher-pupil planned experiences follow a logical sequence of problem solving. The basic objective is to guide the learner in his exploration at every step along the way. Above all, the learner must anticipate each phase of the experience well in advance of the activity and plan accordingly. The procedure which follows is suggestive only.

Identifying the Problem

In teacher-pupil planning, as here conceived, the teacher identifies the problem *area*. He then attempts to develop interest in the area by using such techniques as a discussion, film, resource speaker or oral report. For purposes of illustration, a specific example from the science area is employed. Let us assume that the unit is entitled "Conservation."

> *Creating Interest:* The pupils have read about conservation in their textbooks and weekly newspaper. The suggestion of a day for a field trip to see what they have been studying will create the interest to plan.

Clarifying the Issues

Once the proper foundation has been established, pupils are urged to formulate questions which they would like answered. Emphasis is placed upon realistic, practical problems, rather than upon questions which they think the teacher wants them to ask.

> *Teacher:* From our general study of conservation what subheadings or divisions seem appropriate? What are some areas which might be worthy of exploration?

The class then suggests appropriate groupings. Some of them might be as follows:

1. Identification of conservation practices.
2. Identification of good policies controlling pollution.
3. Identification of poor pollution policies.
4. Can we stop pollution?
5. Ways to aid in conservation.

Teacher: Now, we will list specific questions which you would like to have answered as we study and go on a field trip. Your questions will determine what we will see and study, so make sure they represent what you really want to know. To assist us in organizing our thoughts, we will refer to the general areas listed. Some may develop questions in each area, while others may be interested primarily in only one area.

Questions are grouped and refined. To save time, it may be desirable to appoint a committee for this purpose. When the list of questions has been compiled, the teacher should make copies available to each person.

Planning and Developing the Learning Activities

At this point pupils are assigned to subgroups, usually on the basis of choice. Subgroups of five are preferred. Each subgroup is expected to select a leader and a recorder and to develop a study plan. Each subgroup considers informational sources, along with methods of investigation, reporting, and evaluation. Pupils should give some consideration to all phases of the project so that they can grasp more fully the total task ahead. The teacher moves from group to group, to guide and direct as necessary. For example, pupils may need guidance in rephrasing and expanding some of the questions. "Why do we want to know about the problem of pollution? How can we use the information in our daily lives?" The teacher may find it necessary to assist some groups in developing an appropriate division of labor. Does each person know his specific responsibility? Are the tasks appropriate for the individuals involved?

At the outset the teacher will want to suggest the amount of time available for the project. Time allotments for each group report must be established early. By providing for some flexibility in this respect, pupils are encouraged to use their own imagination relative to unique and creative ways of reporting to the class. They will then need assistance in carrying out such plans.

Collecting Data

The teacher, well in advance of need, should have placed key library references in the classroom, made arrangements for some of the class to be in the library each day, and looked into the possibilities of field trips and other resources.

While investigating a variety of problems, the groups will have different resource needs. These require careful supervision, a great deal of trust in pupils, and a cooperative attitude on the part of other teachers and administrators. The wise teacher will set the stage carefully. The first five minutes of class time might well be devoted to brief progress reports and plans for the day's activities. Copies of the reports should list problems needing attention. The teacher quickly determines which problems need immediate attention. A short class discussion on how to find information may be in order, especially for groups inexperienced in the procedure.

Reporting Procedures

Although a group may have accomplished a great deal in planning and research activities, the value to the class group depends on how well findings are shared with others. Somewhere in the process the entire class might profitably set up standards for this phase of the project. Each group can be asked to consider the problem before planning its specific method of reporting. A master list is then distributed to the chairman of each group. One class listed eight points essential to an appropriate presentation.

1. Material presented should relate to the goals established.
2. Presentations should involve all members of the group in some way.
3. Presentations will be brief, preferably not exceeding fifteen minutes.
4. Presentations should not be read.
5. Other class members should be allotted time for questions. If a

key question cannot be answered, some member of the group should be designated to find the answer.

6. As a general rule, technical material should be omitted from presentations. When it is necessary, however, it should be reproduced for the class.
7. Sources of information should be available.
8. Contradictory evidence should be presented as impartially as possible.

Following each presentation the teacher may lead the class in a general review for the purpose of expanding, clarifying or correcting important points. It is seldom appropriate to have more than two group presentations in one day. However, sometimes keen interest may be indicated, suggesting the desirability of having more group presentations.

Establishing Generalizations

As a culminating activity the teacher will want to conduct a review of the entire project. This will involve recalling the major concepts and procedures employed and expanding to related areas. (See Chapter 16, Review Method.) The activity serves the important function of organizing and clarifying basic ideas which have been developed gradually over a period of several days.

Evaluating the Experience

Early in the cooperative experience, pupils are asked to give some consideration to evaluational techniques. As indicated previously, they assist in establishing standards of reporting. They may want to participate in some sort of group evaluation. Whatever procedure is employed it should be developed jointly by teacher and pupils.

PLANNING FOR THE COOPERATIVE EXPERIENCE

A detailed lesson plan is needed if the teacher-pupil planned project is to develop smoothly. The illustration which follows incorporates the essential steps of the procedure. It is designed to serve for the entire project.

LESSON PLAN ILLUSTRATION (science area—fifth or sixth grade)

Concepts: 1. Conservation helps save our natural resources.
2. Pollution policies may be good or bad depending upon how they affect our environment.
3. Our living habits directly influence the policies concerning conservation and pollution.

Problem: How can we better understand conservation practices and pollution policies?

Goals: After this experience the pupil will know how to identify conservation as evidenced by:

1. His identification of conservation practices he sees on the field trip
2. His group report concerning conservation

After this experience the pupil should have furthered his knowledge of pollution as evidenced by:

1. Identification of pollution he sees on the field trip
2. His group report concerning pollution

After this experience the pupil will understand more fully how to cooperate with others of his peer group in planning as evidenced by:

1. His cooperation during the planning
2. His cooperation and acceptance of responsibility while on the field trip and within his subgroup

Lesson Approach:

CREATING INTEREST:

The pupils have read about conservation in their textbooks and weekly newspaper. The suggestion of a day for a field trip to see what they have been studying will create the interest to plan.

Lesson Development:

TEACHER:

From our general study of conservation what subheadings or divisions seem appropriate? What are some areas which might be worthy of exploration?

The class then suggests five or six groupings. Some of them might be:
1. Identification of conservation practices
2. Identification of good policies controlling pollution
3. Identification of bad pollution policies
4. Ways to stop pollution
5. Ways to aid in conservation

TEACHER:

Now, we will list specific questions which you would like to have answered as we study and go on a field trip. Your questions will determine what we will study, so make sure they represent what you really want to know. To assist us in organizing our thoughts, we will refer to the general areas listed. Some may develop questions in each area, while others may be interested primarily in only one area. (Reproduce question list for each pupil. Add two or three questions if this seems necessary for accomplishment of major objectives.)

FORMULATION OF BUZZ GROUPS:

At this time we will form a separate buzz group for each identified area of our problem for the purpose of correlating our questions. (Ask for volunteers.)

Select a leader and a recorder. List and rework questions, cutting out duplications. *Then* add other questions which are prompted during this activity.

Reproduce question list for each pupil. Add two or three questions if this seems necessary for accomplishment of major objectives.

Development of Learning Activities:

Now that you have studied the list of questions in each area, you see the task before us. We will ask for an indication of preference for committees to be formed for each area.

COMMITTEE BUZZ GROUPS:

Our task is to find the answers to our list of questions and somehow to provide the class with these answers. What are some possible sources of information? (List on chalkboard.) For example:
1. Field trip
2. Books
3. Magazines
4. Resource people

Now let us move into our committees and organize for action, selecting a leader and a recorder. Work out an appropriate division of labor. I will visit each group for the purpose of answering questions.

COLLECTING DATA:

At the conclusion of each day's activities I want you to indicate progress for that day and to suggest problems (if any). Recorder should submit this report after each work period.

Field Trip Standards: What rules of behavior will be established for our field trip? (List.)

Looking Ahead—Anticipating Reporting Techniques: Now that we have had an opportunity to work on our projects for two or three days, let's turn our attention to reporting techniques. What are some possibilities? (List.)   For example:

1. Oral reports
2. Skits
3. Discussion

Standards: What standards should we establish for the presentations? (List.)   For example:

1. Not to be read.
2. Limit to ten minutes long. (Teacher suggests this one.)
3. Separate findings from your own opinions.

Organize for Reporting: At this time you should decide upon a technique(s) for group presentations. Leaders will discuss plans with your teacher, pending final approval.

Evaluation: How should the presentations be evaluated? Let us list some possibilities. (List.)   For example:

1. Teacher rating scales
2. Group evaluation of individuals; class evaluation of groups
3. Written tests

From this list (as groups) decide upon preferences.

Class Presentations: Each individual should list questions as they arise. (Ask during question periods.)

Deriving Generalizations: Now, as a result of our experiences, let us formulate major ideas or concepts which have emerged from these experiences. (List.)   For example:

1. Conservation is everyone's responsibility.
2. Pollution control is important.

VALUES

Teacher-pupil planning is democratically conceived, resulting in increased pupil independence in his own learning activities.

The self-imposed tasks inherent in the procedure result in intrinsic motivation.   Indeed discipline problems are rare if real choices are provided.

The procedure emphasizes *processes* as much as *products* or learning.   Thus
discovery of new ideas and concepts are sought as a *means* of giving
meaning to further performance.

In teacher-pupil planning, cooperative endeavors are emphasized.   Competition tends to shift from individuals to small groups and self-imposed
standards.

The instructional approach emphasizes an active pupil.   Indeed the method
often has been called "project work," calling attention to the inherent
nature of the activities involved.

Development of creativity is encouraged, since the learner must assume
responsibility for solving problems in his own way.

LIMITATIONS AND PROBLEMS

In some areas it is difficult to find legitimate areas of choice.   Especially
in skill areas, a minimum of opportunity for joint teacher-pupil planning activities may be available.

Sometimes individual pupils are not prepared to accept the freedom essential for self-direction.   The break from conformity in learning teacher-
imposed tasks may, on occasion, create anxieties and tensions.   These,
in turn, may be reflected in class misbehavior.   A pattern of gradually
increased responsibilities is usually preferred.

Teachers sometimes lack the ability to relinquish control necessitated by
teacher-pupil planning.   This seems to be the greatest single deterrent
to democratically conceived classes.   Although one is, to a marked
degree, a victim of his own school experiences, the cycle can be broken
by a process of gradually increased pupil involvement.

A criticism occasionally voiced by experienced teachers is the time required
in teacher-pupil planning processes.   Unfortunately, the necessity of
"covering the text or subject" is often implicitly assumed to be the
teacher's basic task.   Today, however, the advancement of knowledge
is expanding at a geometric rate.   Facts soon become outdated.   An
implicit assumption associated with the democratic classroom is the
importance of ideas and concepts in an orderly process of exploration
and discovery.

TEACHER-PUPIL PLANNING ILLUSTRATIONS

I. Useful in the social studies area (primary grades)

Unit: The home

Concepts:

1. All homes have certain similarities.
2. Climate affects the type of homes that are built.
3. Some homes have certain differences.

Problem: How might we understand more about various homes?

Possible areas of interest:

1. Apartment home
2. Single family home
3. Indian home
4. Farm home
5. Trailer home
6. Eskimo home

II. Useful in the reading area (middle grades)

Unit: Oral Reading

Concepts:

1. A child reads orally to share information.
2. Oral reading is a cooperative effort.
3. Good oral reading requires preparation.

Problem: What aspects about oral reading should be explored?

Possible areas of interest:

1. Purposes for oral reading
2. Abilities needed for good oral reading
3. Standards for the oral reader
4. Preparation for oral reading
5. Standards for the audience during oral reading

III. Useful in the health area (upper grades)

Unit: The Human Body

Concepts:

1. A healthy body provides its own defenses against disease.
2. An organ *not* functioning properly tends to influence all body systems.
3. Early diagnosis and treatment of disease are essential.

Problem: What factors about the human body as it fights disease should be explored?

Possible areas of interest:
1. Body defenses against disease
2. Disease influences upon the body
3. Keeping the body healthy
4. Diseased body needs
5. Immunization

13

INQUIRY-DISCOVERY METHOD

The new emphasis upon processes of "inquiry," or "discovery," or "inductive" teaching has created considerable confusion among teachers. Although often referred to as "a method," a perusal of the recent literature suggests many interpretations of meaning. It is generally agreed that the basic processes of inquiry are synonymous with Dewey's steps of reflective thinking, first published around the turn of the century.[1] The "new" emphasis focuses upon pupil self-direction as an outgrowth of a carefully planned situation. *How* a situation may be structured and *how* pupil self-direction may be structured provides most of the apparent confusion over methodology, suggesting not one but many approaches to the problem.

FUNDAMENTAL PROPERTIES

The essence of inquiry, according to Romey,[2] consists of interpretation, generalization, and conclusion. He contends that this is best done in a group discussion. A different point of view holds that the goals of inquiry are designed to reach the pupil as an individual learner.[3]

Although the two *can* be incorporated as a single approach if the

---

[1] John Dewey, *How We Think*, rev. ed. (Boston: D. C. Heath and Co., 1933).

[2] William D. Romey, *Inquiry Techniques for Science* (Englewood Cliffs, N.J.: Prentice-Hall, Inc., 1968).

[3] Vincent R. Rogers, "Anacrocosmic Approach to Inquiry," *Social Education* 70 (January 1970): 74–77.

teacher desires, it should be noted that there are other equally valid approaches to "inquiry" teaching. The major requirement seems to be that of a cooperative experience involving pupil-teacher planning, discussion, conjecture, and attempts at generalization of findings.

The fundamental properties of the inquiry-discovery method are based upon a cooperative experience. This cooperative experience may be teacher-group or teacher-individual situations. In both cases, the classroom environment plays a vital role in the inquiry-discovery method. The fundamental properties of the inquiry-discovery method are treated within this general framework.

Teacher-Group Inquiry

The advocates of teacher-group inquiry feel that *interpretation* is best accomplished in group discussion, based upon a problem designed to encourage pupils to argue. The teacher, as a discussion leader, plays the role of devil's advocate. The class as a group develops its own chain of reasoning as it seeks to *generalize* from the data provided. *Conclusions* are an outgrowth of pupil analysis.

The Individual Learner

Those who favor the teacher-individual cooperative experience suggest that it is the child who must be the active individual in his own learning process in the inquiry-discovery method. The learning activity must be both individualized and personalized to be effective, relevant and enriching to the participant.

A fundamental property of the inquiry-discovery classroom is to provide pupils with an organized, improved method of thinking about and dealing with information. Thus, the learning activities must be provided to allow self-direction for the pupil. Thus, each individual has some topic, problem or question to investigate that has high interest appeal and about which he is curious. Findings, of course, are shared and evaluated by the entire class group.

Classroom Environment

A fundamental property of the inquiry-discovery method is a classroom climate that is open to queries. The children in the classroom must feel comfortable in asking questions. Each child should have the assurance that the teacher and his classmates will listen and respect his questions and discovery activities.

The teacher must establish an environment in the classroom that will stimulate curiosity. He should provide a wide range of experiences in which the pupil is involved with concrete objects, printed materials, pictorial items, audiovisual devices, creative and investigative activities.

Problem Focused

A fundamental aspect of the inquiry-discovery method is that it focuses on problems. These problems are defined and probed. Often in the inquiry method, the problems have the possibility of more than one correct answer. In working through the problem there is more than one way of arriving at answers; therefore, a range of alternatives is always possible for the pupil.

Questions Stressed

In the inquiry-discovery method, questions are stressed rather than answers. Questions become the important aspect of the teaching act and they are used to find out what the pupil knows and does not know. In addition, questions are asked to arouse interest, evaluate a pupil's preparation, develop insights, review and summarize materials, stimulate critical thinking, and evaluate the achievement of goals.

INQUIRY-DISCOVERY PROCEDURE

The inquiry-discovery procedure may vary somewhat from one situation to another; however, the major objective is to develop a cooperative experience in which the child is encouraged to explore, experiment, and discover facts, generalizations, and techniques. Preparation and planning, initiating activity, development of the lesson, concept development, and evaluating the pupil behavior are all necessary steps in the inquiry-discovery procedure.

Preparation and Planning

In planning for the inquiry-discovery process, the teacher must carefully select an area to be explored. He collects documents and other objects, places books in the classroom, and arranges for full use of the available resources. If maps, diagrams, pictures, tables, and art objects are anticipated, he must have resources available when needed.

In addition to getting the classroom environment ready for the inquiry-discovery process, the teacher must develop his behavioral objectives, questioning strategies, and planning activities well in advance of the lesson.

Initiating the Activity

Quite frequently the project is introduced with a "discovery episode" which serves as a springboard for inquiry and discussion. Be it a short poem in language arts or a short science demonstration, the objective is to stimulate thinking.

Four types of discovery episodes are described by Esler.[4] There is the *discrepant event* which offends the senses of the observer. This may involve an unexpected outcome of a physical event such as two glasses of clear liquid in which an ice cube is placed in each. The ice cube floats in the one glass and not the other. Another approach involves an *anecdote with a demonstration*. To illustrate: A teacher may tell (as he demonstrates) of a boy or girl who, while drinking a soft drink, fills the opening around the straw with bubble gum and soon finds it is no longer possible to draw the drink up the straw. A third approach may involve an *anecdote without a demonstration*. Here the teacher merely presents a problem situation and directs an inquiry session wherein pupils attempt a solution. A fourth type of discovery episode, frequently used in such subjects as mathematics and social studies, is a *pictorial stimulator*. By presenting data in chart, graph or table form (minus explanatory notes), inquiry attempts can be aimed at interpreting data and drawing conclusions.

[4] W. K. Esler, "Structured Inquiry for Classroom Use," *School Science and Mathematics* 70 (May 1970): 545–548.

Development of the Lesson

The discussion episode is used to further develop the lesson and to induce perplexity and to create the general attitude that the teacher is also an inquirer who has no absolute answers to offer. It is emphasized that points must be defended on the basis of data. This sets the stage for group work that follows. In short, the teacher prods pupils to explore and test new alternatives. Questions usually are redirected to the group. During time of impasses, he may raise additional questions, designed to help pupils see alternative ways of resolving an issue. Sometimes the pupil-question, teacher-answer technique may be employed. To refrain from supplying too much information, pupils may be restricted to questions that may be answered by "yes" or "no."

The inquiry-oriented teacher encourages pupils "to play their hunches" and to conjecture. He considers this activity to be the core of classroom instruction. Generally, the teacher's role may be described as dialectical rather than didactic, inasmuch as it is assumed that pupils will learn more when provided opportunities to discover ideas and relationships for themselves.[5]

During the development of the lesson, the pupils are expected to ask questions, formulate hypotheses, search for additional data, draw conclusions, and learn concepts. Concept formulation may be learned by grouping or classifying those facts that have common properties, labeling each group, listing specific pieces of information from a larger whole or by generalizing from the facts presented. From the conclusions developed by an individual child or a group of children, a concept could also be formulated. During the inquiry-discovery method, concepts are not only learned, but must be put to use in observing, classifying, generalizing, and other processes.

Evaluation

The evaluation of the process of inquiry-discovery should be continuous. Throughout this method, the teacher should observe how each child goes about his task of inquiry as well as the end product of his work. Inasmuch as the inquiry-discovery method is a cooperative activity, much of the evaluation can be done through joint pupil-teacher evaluation.

[5] Byron G. Massialas and Jack Zevin, *Creative Encounters in the Classroom: Teaching and Learning Through Discovery* (New York: John Wiley and Sons, Inc., 1967), p. 26.

Pupil behavior that can be evaluated would include the type of questions the child asks, how well the pupil identifies problems, how he organizes information, and how well he can proceed through the inquiry-discovery process to a hypothesis and concept.

PLANNING FOR INQUIRY-DISCOVERY

A major problem that causes poor inquiry-discovery lessons is the lack of planning on the part of the teacher. One of the greatest changes a teacher should make when using this method is in his preparation and planning. The illustrated lesson plan presents only a guide to an inquiry-discovery classroom experience. Many other approaches to this method could be just as appropriate.

LESSON PLAN ILLUSTRATION (Science—fifth or sixth grade).

Unit: Matter—Its Changes

Concepts: 1. Matter has different volume depending upon its state.
2. Atmospheric pressure is exerted upon matter.
3. Heat can be conducted.
4. Vapor exerts a pressure.

Problem: Does matter change its volume when it changes its state?

Goals: After this lesson the pupil should have furthered his understanding of one of the above science concepts, as evidenced by:

1. His ability to identify the problem through asking questions
2. His ability to organize information
3. His ability to develop a hypothesis
4. His ability to generalize and learn a concept

Initiating the Activity: The Discovery Episode

"What do you see here on the science table?"

(The following responses may be made by the pupils.)

"A can with a screw-down cap."
"A Bunsen burner."
"A beaker of water."

"I am putting one inch of water in the can. Now as I heat the can with the water in it, what will happen?"

(The pupils may give various responses.)

When the water begins to boil, the cap is screwed on tightly. After the water has boiled and the cap is secured tightly, a stream of cold water will be poured over the can. The can will then collapse.

Lesson Development: The Discussion Episode. Some possible questions are as follows:

1. Why did the can collapse?
2. Why was it necessary to put water in the can?
3. Why was the can heated?
4. Why did the can need to be capped?
5. Why was it necessary to pour cold water over the can?

(During this time questions usually are redirected to the group.)

Deriving Generalizations or Concepts: From the demonstration, what big ideas seem to stand out? For example:

1. For the walls of the can to move inward, it is necessary that forces pushing in be greater than the forces pushing out.
2. The atmospheric pressure pushing in on the can is constant throughout the experiment; therefore, the forces pushing outward must have decreased.
3. When water changes into steam, the volume is increased.

VALUES

In the inquiry-discovery method the pupil assumes the central role in the educative process. He becomes an active inquirer rather than a passive learner.

Emphasis is upon problems which are defined, probed, and labeled as relevant to the learner.

The inquiry-discovery method's aim is the development of judgment-making ability. A range of alternatives is always available.

In effect, the method shifts the role of the teacher from that of supplying answers to one of asking questions.

Every individual's belief system of values and attitudes is considered important. Expanding and developing that system is a major goal.

The teacher, too, is an inquirer. At no time does he assume to know all that is being learned.

Emphasis upon competition for grades is removed. The pupil is working with goals that are his own.

LIMITATIONS AND PROBLEMS

In a group inquiry-discovery session, not all pupils may be involved in the actual process. One pupil may make all the decisions and another pupil may merely record the decisions.

There is a danger that the inquiry-discovery method may become a ritual rather than a true problem-solving approach.

The time factor is an important aspect in the inquiry-discovery method. There is a decided tendency to "rush" pupil responses. Critical thinking takes time.

There is a tendency with some pupils to provide answers or solutions to problems which the pupil feels is the teacher's preconceived solution. Sometimes such a session may evolve into a "game" to ascertain what the teacher has in mind.

ILLUSTRATED INQUIRY-DISCOVERY PROBLEMS

I. Useful in the social studies area (primary grades)

   Unit: Community Helpers

   Concept: Policemen are needed in our community.

   Problem: Why are policemen needed in our community?

   Discovery Episode: From a picture of a policeman, the following questions may be developed:

   1. What do they do?
   2. Why do they carry a gun?

3. What might happen if our community did not have them?
4. What makes a good policeman?

II. Useful in the study skills area (middle grades)

Unit: Map Reading

Concept: Geographic features and natural resources affect the growth and location of cities.

Problem: Where should the largest city be placed on this map?

Discovery Episode: After reading various maps of the same area, each pupil may develop the following questions for inquiry:
1. How will rivers and lakes affect the size of cities?
2. How will mountains, valleys, and other land forms affect the growth of cities?
3. How will climate affect the city size?
4. How will mineral deposits affect the size of the city?

III. Useful in the reading area (any grade)

Unit: Critical Reading

Concept: Drawing conclusions from facts read are processes of critical reading.

Problem: How could this story end?

Discovery Episode: After reading a third of a selection, the following speculative questions may be developed:
1. What inferences can be drawn from the reading?
2. What conclusions can be made from the material read?
3. What could be the story plot?
4. What is the likely outcome for the story?

IV. Useful in the health area (upper grades)

Unit: Foods Useful for Man

Concept: Modern technology has made it possible for people to eat food grown in all parts of the world.

Problem: How is modern technology changing people's eating habits?

Discovery Episode: After viewing a filmstrip about technology and food, the following questions may be developed:
1. Why are some kinds of foods grown in some areas of the world and not in other areas?

2. What would happen if the transportation system of today stopped immediately?
3. How can technology make it possible to eat food from all areas of the world?
4. Why can food be produced in an area which does *not* have the proper geographic requirements?
5. Why does the availability of food make a difference in people's eating habits?

14

ORAL REPORTING TECHNIQUES

Strictly speaking, there is no single oral reporting method. Rather, the term encompasses several allied techniques. When the teacher or pupil informs others by telling, explaining or showing, this is oral reporting. The traditional (formal) lecture method, first popularized in the medieval university, was designed as the basic instructional approach for a school system which emphasized knowledge as an instructional end. As emphasis shifted from the acquisition of knowledge for its own sake to the *use* of knowledge to solve meaningful life problems, the formal lecture fell into disrepute.

Oral reporting in the elementary school is designed to expedite pupil problem-solving activities. It may be employed for varying lengths of time at any point in the learning process when it becomes obvious that pupils can profit from outside assistance. Frequently oral reports are used to provide pupils with essential background information for subsequent learning experiences. Often the procedure will involve use of certain films or demonstrations.

FUNDAMENTAL PROPERTIES

There is nothing sacred per se about the size of a class group in which a pupil learns. Learning results in a combination of listening, viewing, reading, and talking activities. The size of a group is most appropriately determined by the purposes or objectives being sought. Likewise, the choice of instructional method will depend upon what must be accomplished. It has been assumed throughout this book that the bulk of major learning activities should be so organized as to accommodate critical thinking. The fundamental properties of oral reporting are treated within this general framework.

Objectivity

In evaluating evidence the learner must have access to the pertinent facts. Since the teacher, pupil or resource person may represent the major source of information, an objective, unbiased presentation is essential. The demonstrator or reporter must clearly label private opinions if they must be stated. He will state his knowledge sources and indeed will encourage further investigation when controversy is evident. Whenever possible, a report is avoided in highly controversial areas.

Visual Aids

Oral presentations are difficult to understand and to remember unless supplemented liberally with visual aids. Use of the chalkboard, pictures, color transparencies, diagrams, and the like can greatly enhance effectiveness of oral presentations. An effective reporter, for example, frequently outlines his major points on the chalkboard or chart and then proceeds to develop each point by offering numerous illustrations and examples. With the use of visual aids, the pupils are better able to remember and understand the main ideas in the report.

Repetition

Repetition provides another useful means of supplementing the spoken word. It is characterized by an initial summary, periodic summaries along the way (if the oral report is of considerable length), and a final summary. A teacher once expressed the idea in these words: "Tell your listeners what you plan to say, tell them, and then tell them what you have said." Such planned repetition seems more vivid, thereby providing a much needed structure for retention of major points.

Feedback

Feedback is an essential aspect of the instructional process. Teachers quite naturally accept and sometimes elicit questions during difficult explanations. Teacher or pupil oral reports and demonstrations are usually short, providing opportunities for clarifications immediately after the experiences. Sometimes the question period may even exceed the length of the original presentation. It is only through such feedback that the reporter or demonstrator is able to discover blocks to communication and learning.

Supplementary Techniques

When learning is conceived as a process of critical thinking, it is obvious that the oral report cannot stand alone. Psychologists have emphasized repeatedly the importance of an overtly active learner. Whenever the oral report is employed, it merely serves the function of providing data and background information needed for resolution of an important problem. Thus the oral report must be supplemented with additional learning activities germane to a given problem.

Time Limitations

The elementary school age is an active one. The pupils usually experience difficulty in concentrating on a problem for a long time. They need to move about, to ask questions, to express themselves frequently. Thus oral presentations should be limited to a period of not more than ten to fifteen minutes. With small children, even the teacher has difficulty keeping the children's interest over fifteen minutes. Even so, they must be interspersed with extended periods of activity. If the oral report must be longer, it should be broken into two time periods, separated with a lively question and answer session.

ORAL REPORTING PROCEDURE

As has been indicated, oral reporting procedures vary somewhat from one situation to another. For example, a report or demonstration may vary from one or two minutes of spontaneous explanation to an entire class period. The frame of reference utilized in this section is the preplanned presentation (by the teacher or by the pupil) which usually ranges from ten to fifteen minutes. Generally the procedure will incorporate the essentials of oral reporting and demonstration procedures. Important differences in these techniques are noted.

Identifying the Problem

The oral report problem usually is formulated as a question of fact. Such problems are characterized as "is" or "are" questions. A fifth grade pupil, for example, might be asked to prepare an oral report on the American buffalo. When formulated as a question of fact, the problem might be: "What factors contributed to the virtual extinction of the American buffalo (bison)?" Although oral reports often are assigned as topics, pupils limit and clarify problems by formulating specific factual-type questions.

Problems of a highly controversial nature usually are not handled as oral reports. Sometimes a teacher will find it necessary to report on such a problem, but he must present different points of view as objectively as possible.

Organizing the Presentation

Oral techniques are ineffective unless the speaker captures the imagination of the listeners. He can do this by beginning his presentation with an unusual or startling statement. One pupil, for example, who was reporting the effects of fluoridation on teeth began his presentation with, "I hate dental appointments."

When the topic is of considerable interest to the group, one may go into it directly. This is best accomplished by reference to the main theme or purpose. For example, the teacher who finds it necessary to interrupt other class activities to give a needed explanation usually will plunge directly into the points to be clarified. Many times, however, the group will not be especially concerned with the subject. They may not understand how a presentation relates to the ongoing class activities. Most reports and demonstrations fall into this category. In addition to a catchy title, designed to arouse curiosity, an *attention-getting* opening is needed. A startling statement, question or unusual illustration at the very beginning can gain immediate attention. The pupil who was to present a report on the effects of fluoridation on teeth might open his talk with these words:

> Your teeth are as old as a thirty year old man. A man who has lived thirty years has lived almost one-half of his life; a tooth which has lived twelve years has lived approximately one-half of its life. But with the help of fluoridation the average tooth may chew well for you. . . .

The pupil cited above made an unusual comparison. Then, while attention was high, he indicated how his information could be of value to his listeners.

The attention and needs set the stage for that which is to follow. Usually three or four statements will suffice. The speaker must carefully avoid extending this part of his presentation beyond its usefulness.

It is in the *satisfaction* phase of a presentation that one states his references and presents the main points of his talk. The individual can greatly increase the effectiveness of this phase of his presentation by adhering to a simple outline.

1. *Initial summary.* This consists of a brief enumeration of the main points to be made. For young people especially, it is desirable to write these points on the chalkboard.
2. *Detailed information.* Here the speaker brings in supporting facts, examples, and illustrations to clarify the issues. It is desirable to show the relationship between the major points.

   Some individuals have difficulty in determining what the main points will be. The reporter can consider breaking his topic into such categories as time sequence (past, present, future), cause and effect relationships, interested parties involved, anticipated problems and their solutions, and topical arrangement.

   The speaker completes his discussion of a point before proceeding to the next one. By referring to the original points listed on the chalkboard, he is able to move from one area to another without losing his listeners.
3. *Final summary.* The speaker concludes by restating his main points and important conclusions which have been developed.

The pupil who reported on the effects of fluoridation on teeth broke his presentation into three parts—causes of tooth decay, effects of fluoridation, and permanence of fluoridation treatment. After placing his main points on the board for the benefit of the class, he presented facts and examples designed to clarify each of the main points.

Listening Techniques

One of the most difficult problems facing a teacher involves ways and means of educating a group to listen effectively. It is easy enough to spot the pupil who is overtly disturbing, but much of the time it is practically impossible to detect the individual who has let his mind wander to more pleasing avenues of thought. On the other hand, some individuals who attempt to listen carefully have difficulty forming the mental images essential for comprehension.

In many life situations, listening is voluntary or purposeful. Often this is not the case in ordinary classroom situations. Many times members of the audience are captive listeners. (In most states, youngsters are required to attend school and participate in programs in which they have no genuine interest.) Attention, however, is enhanced *when the listener realizes that he is to become directly involved in subsequent activities*. For example:

1. A teacher explained an arithmetic problem, involving principles necessary for doing the assignment.
2. The teacher issued final instructions before the start of an extended field trip.
3. Mary gave a report on the mountain rattlesnake which the group was likely to encounter on a science excursion.
4. An individual demonstrated techniques of artificial respiration prior to practice by each pupil.

Listening is also enhanced when the speaker is sincerely interested in what he is saying. Frequently this is lacking in assigned reports. The pupil may see his task as just a job to be done. The speaker who makes his presentation almost a life or death matter is likely to hold his listeners.

Pupils listen better when a presentation appeals to basic motives. All people have certain basic physical and psychological drives or desires. It has been established that the need for social approval, self-preservation, affection, integrity, pleasure, and the like exist in varying degrees within all human beings. The reporter or demonstrator is more likely to interest his audience if he identifies his subject with one or more of these needs. To accomplish this end, however, he must project himself into the shoes of his listeners. At some point in the process the speaker replaces his own motives with those of his listeners.

Thus far, consideration has been given to the speaker's efforts to gain attention of his audience. However, communication is a joint process between the speaker and the observer. The listener himself has definite responsibilities, other than merely placing himself within hearing range of the speaker and assuming the proper listening pose.

One who listens pays attention to what is being said, that is, he is "at-tension." This state of mind suggests that one is focusing his faculties on what he expects to receive from the experience. He *listens with a purpose*. The person who listens in a vague sort of way is likely to receive little benefit from the presentation. In an expository type of presentation the hearer is interested in the soundness and relationships of the facts and ideas presented. This, in turn, will help him organize his listening for a purpose. After all, there will always be reports and demonstrations which are poorly organized. However, it may still be possible to profit from the experience, despite the speaker's limitations.

Presenting the Oral Report

The effective presentation of an oral report or demonstration adheres to all the characteristics of effective speaking. First of all, the speaker must be heard. He needs to vary his voice in such a way as to drive home his points. The good speaker is enthusiastic about what he has to say; he looks directly at his listeners—talking "to" them rather than "at" them.

Techniques of delivery will be found in almost any basic speech textbook. The following elements of effective communication are basic:

1. He speaks in a conversational manner.
2. He thinks as he talks and talks as he thinks.
3. He closely observes audience reactions.
4. He maintains poise at all times. (Some teachers violate this rule by sitting on the desk or leaning on a speaker's stand. In an attempt to appear casual or relaxed, they appear to some pupils as sloppy or lazy.)
5. He avoids annoying mannerisms. (One may develop little habits which detract seriously from what is being said. Often the teacher is unaware of these annoyances. Some teachers periodically provide pupils an opportunity to indicate the nature and extent of such annoying mannerisms. Anonymity is essential for valid suggestions.)

Entertaining Questions

The question or discussion period following an oral report or demonstration is of utmost importance. The report, being designed to inform the group, usually needs some clarification. This can come only from the group, as the speaker cannot know the type of mental images his discourse has produced. Three to five minutes usually will suffice for a fifteen minute report.

The teacher then leads the class in a brief *review* of the main points made and brings them to bear upon the solution of a problem. The reader will recall that an oral report is meant to be a *basis* for problem solving. It is concerned with the data-gathering (factual) step. There remains the evaluation of the data and their bearing upon an appropriate solution of the problem under consideration. In the process of review both pupils and teacher can bring related information to bear upon the problem.

A concomitant outcome of an oral report can be valuable training in evaluation of data. Pupils need training in assessing the validity and reliability of both the spoken and written word. Fallacies, improper deduction, and outright distortion of facts are among the most prevalent weaknesses of oral reports. Young pupils, especially, are prone to confuse the issues by expressing their own value judgments along with the facts.

Most demonstrations are performed to help pupils visualize how conclusions are reached. Frequently the class is expected to form certain conclusions on the basis of evidence produced by the demonstration. Teachers violate sound scientific principles, however, by encouraging pupils to conclude too much on the basis of *one* experiment.

Evaluating Oral Presentations

To assist pupils, especially the older elementary school children, in improving their oral reporting techniques, an evaluation is an essential ingredient. However, one of the most difficult and controversial aspects of oral presentations involves evaluation. Indeed, some teachers attempt to judge such presentations on the basis of purely general impressions. Some authorities would seriously question or even deplore such a technique. Whether or not we like it, evaluations of oral discourses are highly subjective. Thus they are affected by certain predispositions of the evaluator. The personal factor involved can be substantially reduced by establishing a number of bases for such an evaluation.

At least three bases which can be used are the following:

1. A presentation can be judged on the basis of the response of the group. Do pupils seem interested in the report during the actual presentation? Are there a number of appropriate questions following the report? Do pupils keep referring to the speaker's points in the follow-through session?
2. A presentation can be evaluated on the basis of the techniques of presentation. Was there evidence of planning or of proper body and voice control? Was eye contact maintained throughout?
3. A report can be judged on the basis of the adequacy of content coverage. Did the speaker present the facts fully? Was he able to maintain his role as impartial observer?

The fallacy of using audience reaction as a sole basis for evaluation is readily apparent. Many reportorial topics, for instance, may provoke enthusiasm because they are of immediate concern to the group. Or they may happen to support previous convictions of many of the listeners. Sometimes the reporter himself will be especially well liked by the group. Enthusiasm expressed under such circumstances can be high, even though the content is poorly stated or even invalid.

The immediate disadvantage of relying solely on techniques of delivery is inherent in the purpose of the talk. A report is designed to inform a group of people. Although recommended speech techniques correlate with effective communication, it is possible that the criterion of objective techniques will not be an effective measure for a particular individual.

The third criterion for evaluating a report is the adequacy of the content. The completeness and accuracy of content can be lost if oral communication is ineffective; therefore, the report *cannot* be judged solely on facts presented. The oral report is dependent on adequate communication of ideas.

It can be seen, then, that all three bases of evaluation are needed. Few teachers can maintain a very high degree of accuracy by relying on general impressions only. Many teachers utilize rating scales which can be checked during and immediately following oral presentations.

The Rating Scale for Oral Presentations, which follows, illustrates the essentials of such a measure. It will be noted that all three of the bases for evaluation described above are included in the rating scale. In addition, there is a dimension for "general effectiveness." Different teachers, of course, favor different evaluation forms.

RATING SCALE FOR ORAL PRESENTATIONS

DIRECTIONS: Pupil will be marked with a check (√) on a continuum from one end of the line to the other. A check within the broken lines will be roughly equivalent to an average rating.

I. Delivery.

    A. Lesson Beginning.

Attention-getting, indicative of general content.	Beginning apparently planned, but effectiveness somewhat lacking.	Beginning poorly given; rambling statements; apologies.

    B. Audience Contact.

Looks directly at his listeners.	Depends heavily on notes, apparently does not "see" his listeners.	Reads from notes or looks above heads of listeners.

    C. Enthusiasm.

Intensely interested in topic. Stress is "natural" or "spontaneous."	Some interest evident. Occasionally lapses into a monotone.	Lack of interest; just another job to be done.

    D. Use of Communication Skills (voice, posture and gestures, grammar, spelling, penmanship).

Communication skills above reproach.	One or two of the communication skills need further development.	Several communication skills need immediate attention.

II. Content.

    A. Major Points.

Major points stressed and supported with pertinent examples.	Major points not very clearly defined and developed.	Content of the presentation confusing or extremely vague.

    B. Objectivity.

Distinguishes between "facts" and opinion.	Sometimes difficult to distinguish between facts and opinion. Tends to over-emphasize own opinions.	Facts and opinions generally indistinguishable. Apparently unaware of projections.

III. Audience Reaction.

Pupils attentive and ask pertinent questions.	Some audience interest evident. Questions are brief.	Little evidence of interest. Few questions.

IV. General Effectiveness.

High over-all effectiveness. Appropriate "balance" maintained.	Presentation reasonably effectively.	Presentation generally ineffective. Lacks needed "punch."

PLANNING FOR THE ORAL REPORT

Techniques of informing others must be carefully planned. Pupils are painfully aware of teachers who "cannot explain very well" or those who "are confusing or difficult to follow." Likewise, pupils and teachers recognize the difficulties that many pupils experience when asked to present oral reports. Most of these difficulties are related to inadequate planning. It is hoped that the illustrated plan which follows will clarify the problem somewhat. The plan is suggestive only.

LESSON PLAN ILLUSTRATION (useful in the health area—fifth or sixth grade)

> *Concept:*   The outer, middle, and inner ear are involved in conducting sound waves as we hear.
>
> *Problem:*   What are the functions of the outer, middle, and inner ear?
>
> *Goals:*   After this lesson, the pupil should further understand how we hear, as evidenced by:
>   1. His ability to relate the function of the outer, middle, and inner ear
>   2. The questions he asks in the subsequent discussion: What are the functions of the outer, middle, and inner ear?
>   3. His application of the basic demonstration concepts to a subsequent pictorial drawing

Lesson Approach:

1. *Attention Getting:*   (Pop a balloon.)   Did you hear something?   How does one hear the pop?   All of us hear something all the time; so we seem to take hearing for granted.
2. *Initial Summary:*   How we hear is dependent upon the function of the outer ear, the middle ear, and the inner ear. (Write these three on the chalkboard: 1. Outer Ear, 2. Middle Ear, and 3. Inner Ear.)   Sound waves are necessary for us to hear, too.

Lesson Development:

1. *Slides and transparencies.*   Through the use of slides and transparencies show how waves and frequency play their part in hearing.

2. *Tuning fork.* Discuss sound vibrations per second.
3. *Show ear model.* Use the model of the ear to demonstrate the various parts of the ear and their function.

Deriving Generalizations: From the foregoing demonstration a number of generalizations seem evident. These are a few illustrations:

1. Sound vibrations (waves) moving through the air are received by the ear.
2. The ear is divided into three separate sections—the outer ear, the middle ear, and the inner ear.
3. The outer ear catches sound waves from the air.
4. When sound waves strike the outer surface of the eardrum, it vibrates and these vibrations are mechanically transmitted through the middle ear.
5. The round window membrane transmits vibrations into the inner ear.
6. Vibrations in the inner ear are received by nerve cells that carry the impulses to the brain.

The foregoing lesson plan is more detailed than many teachers prefer; perhaps it is not detailed enough for others. The primary purpose of this plan is to provide information not readily accessible. The information is useful (along with other facts) in providing a factual *basis* for resolving fundamental issues in the health area. Certain aspects of the demonstration undoubtedly touched upon in text materials were *reorganized* and re-presented. These aspects, of course, merely would be mentioned in the presentation.

VALUES

Oral reporting is economical in terms of time and materials.
The method serves to channel thinking of all pupils in a given direction.
Demonstrations enable the teacher to utilize activities which would be too dangerous for pupils themselves to perform within the ordinary classroom.
Oral reports and demonstrations are easy to prepare, as they are usually based on specialized knowledge of the leader.

LIMITATIONS AND PROBLEMS

Information-giving methods can encourage the retention of facts as ends in themselves.

The method, in and of itself, is inadequate for teaching certain types of concepts. (Attitudes, feelings, and skills, for example, are not learned through pure telling or showing procedures.)

Some teachers have difficulty adapting their presentations to the comprehension levels of their pupils. (A passive audience is less able to indicate its lack of understanding.)

Social learnings are minimized during oral presentations.

This approach to teaching tends to encourage acceptance of the teacher as a final authority. In this way a teacher's bias and prejudices may be accepted at face value.

Exposition processes are extremely difficult to adapt to individual differences of pupils. Superior pupils, for example, frequently complain of boredom "after about the fifth explanation." Likewise, less able pupils often charge that oral reports go "too fast."

ILLUSTRATED ORAL REPORT OUTLINES

I. Useful in the science area (primary grades)

Unit: Space

Concept: Oceans occupy space.

Problem: How large a space do oceans occupy?

Main Points:

1. Ocean basins are very large.
2. If all the land above the sea was pushed into the ocean basin, it would not be filled.
3. The Pacific Ocean basin is believed to be almost the same size as the moon.

II. Useful in the social studies area (middle grades)

Unit: Construction

Concept: The construction engineers build dams for many reasons.

Problem: What are the reasons for building dams?

Main Points:

1. Dams are used to prevent floods.
2. Dams are built to conserve water.
3. Through the use of dams, power and energy can be developed.

III. Useful in the reading area (upper grades)

Unit: Reading Comprehension

Concept: The good reader must perform specific activities while reading.

Problem: What must a reader do to comprehend and read well?

Main Points:

1. A good reader must remember the essentials of what is read.
2. A good reader relates the details to main ideas.
3. A good reader is able to place story events in a proper sequence.
4. A good reader understands the author through literal and/or interpretive comprehension activities.

IV. Useful in the arithmetic area (middle grades)

Unit: Approximating and Estimating

Concept: Estimation is used to avoid gross errors in arithmetic problems.

Problem: What method can you use to avoid making gross errors in arithmetic problems?

Main Points:

1. An estimate of the answer is made before computation.
2. An estimate is a close guess.
3. After the computation, the answer and estimate are compared.
4. Estimates are used as a quick way to determine whether or not an answer is too small or too large.

V. Useful in language arts area (middle and upper grades)

Unit: Oral Language

Concept: Standards for giving reports will increase the effectiveness of oral reports.

Problem: What are the standards for reporting in the classroom?

Main Points:

1. Speak to the entire class.
2. Speak so everyone in the class can hear.
3. Stay on the topic for the report.
4. Use gestures and movements when necessary.
5. Use visual aids to enhance the report.
6. Mention where you read or acquired the information.
7. Use proper and correct language.
8. Do *not* use run-together sentences.

15

FILM ANALYSIS METHOD

Almost all teachers make use of motion pictures. Too often, however, educational films have been misused. Although a film may create considerable interest, there is no assurance that a film used alone will result in any worthwhile learnings. Since it is necessarily an abstraction, designed to highlight selected elements of reality, *misconceptions* are all too common.

Like dramatic play and simulation games (treated in Chapters 10 and 11), a film is a simulation of reality. As such, it is ideally suited for capturing time and space problems. As with other instructional methods, the learner must be guided in appropriate processes of critical thinking. The film analysis which follows is suggestive only. Its use is limited to those films which are designed to develop basic instructional concepts.

FUNDAMENTAL PROPERTIES

Although some educational films have been used by enterprising teachers for many years, the full impact of their value is just beginning to be realized by the great majority of teachers. Certainly the unbelievably rapid progress in the direction of automation has been felt. In some cases, increased use of instructional materials has become a fad. However, the major impact of educational films can be attributed to a new concept of the final goal of education. Teachers are beginning to realize

163

that "the final goal of education is not memorized information; it is a changed individual, who lives differently because he has learned."[1]

Teacher's Role

An educational system which hopes to change behavior must do much more than provide facts. It must deal with personal perceptions —with individual meaning. Meanings exist within each individual and cannot be manipulated or controlled. Thus the teacher's role becomes one of helping youngsters explore and discover for themselves the personal meaning of events in films. The teacher's task, then, is one of creating a favorable climate for learning. Bridging the gap of time and space for *personal meaning* often demands the use of films.

Single Concept Films

At the present time three types of films are available for class use: single concept films, documentaries, and sponsored films. The *single concept film*, of recent origin, is usually short—ranging from three to fifteen minutes in length. Like other simulations, its function is to introduce a problem without attempting to solve it.

Documentary Films

The *documentary film* is designed to portray the everyday world in a manner to emphasize relationships and meaning. Its aim is to provide new insights and new understandings, but it does express a given point of view. Several documentary films appearing on television screens today, for example, depict life in the ghetto. Others are designed especially for those contemplating extended vacation trips.

Sponsored Films

The *sponsored film* is commercially produced for the purpose of presenting a given point of view. Some such films may be produced as

---

[1] Edgar Dale, *Audiovisual Methods in Teaching*, 3rd ed. (New York: Holt, Rinehart and Winston, Inc., 1969), p. 24. For a comprehensive and practical treatment of audiovisual materials, the reader will find Dale's book most helpful.

a part of broad advertising and public relations program. The advertising message does not necessarily render such a film inappropriate for class use. In fact, some commercial film producers design films especially for class use, their major purpose being to inform. Nevertheless, they should be previewed carefully for bias and distortions.

FILM UTILIZATION PROCEDURE

A film is designed to further an educational objective. After the teacher has identified the major concepts to be taught, he proceeds to develop activities which may assist in accomplishing this end. Being aware of the best films in his field and having access to latest film catalogs are essential parts of film analysis.

Preplanning

The teacher must arrange to preview those films which may serve his purposes. Today most schools have special facilities available for this function. A critique of every film previewed, whether used or not, is useful for future reference. A preview is essential to the development of an adequate film analysis.

Effective timing is another critical aspect of preplanning. At what point during the instructional process should a film be introduced? Some films, for example, are most effectively used to introduce a lesson, others should be used as or along with the heart of a lesson, a few may be useful as culmination activities.

Scheduling the Film

Usually films must be scheduled several days in advance. How is one to predict precise progress of pupils? Obviously, this is an impossibility! About all the teacher can do is to predict as accurately as possible and then adjust accordingly. Some schools are producing their own single concept films as one way of overcoming some of the timing problems. Sometimes a film does not arrive as scheduled. Occasionally a film projector breaks down and so on. Thus, it is imperative that alternative activities be prepared for every scheduled use of a film. This is not a particularly difficult task but one that is frequently neglected by many teachers.

Introducing the Film

The introductory comments preceding the showing of a film are designed to prepare the pupils for the experience. Usually two or three key questions should be posed. Rather than emphasizing facts, the questions should focus upon relationships, application or hidden meaning. Sometimes certain problems or problem situations should be noted. At other times, new terms or new ideas should be pinpointed. Too many questions or points to look for may be confusing.

Normally, key points to look for in a film are put on the board for further reference. Pupils should be discouraged from taking notes during the showing of a film. A film may be stopped for emphasis and discussion; it may be rerun in slow motion.

Follow-Through Discussion

The first step in the follow-through discussion is to determine how well the original questions or problems can be answered. This leads to resolution of the problem. As with any other method, various possible solutions should be posed and evaluated. If a single concept film is used this is a natural outgrowth of the experience. If a documentary or sponsored film is utilized, considerable guidance may be necessary.

Attention must be directed to incorrect notions or unanticipated misunderstandings which may have resulted. Sometimes differences between the film and information from other sources may conflict or at least appear to do so. Above all, pupils should be encouraged to pose their own questions for reflection. Sometimes pupil questions will suggest the need for a second showing of the film, or they may suggest the need for other class activities.

Deriving Generalizations

As a culmination of the learning experience, the derivation of ideas or generalizations should be encouraged. These may evolve from the film itself, or they may be an outgrowth of activities which may have preceded or followed the film. If film bias is noted, this will become a part of the summation activities.

PLANNING FOR THE FILM

Audiovisual materials and resources are so common and so varied that little effort has been made to specify specific uses. Several aids, such as the chalkboard, the overhead projector, still pictures, and the like are used as tools to enhance the instructional effectiveness of other methods and techniques. Films also find their place in this manner. Frequently, however, a film represents the method itself. There is an all too common tendency to assume that the film itself can teach. *When used as an instructional method, a film must be planned within a framework of problem solving.* The lesson plan which follows is based upon a single concept film. Such films are ideally suited for this purpose.

LESSON PLAN ILLUSTRATION (useful in the reading area—primary grades)

Unit: Abraham Lincoln

Concept: Honesty is an essential part of a person's character.

Problem: What policy should one follow when one finds money that belongs to someone else?

Goals: After this lesson, the pupil should have furthered his ability to perceive the relationship between honesty and dishonesty, as evidenced by:
1. His comments and questions during the follow-through discussion of a single concept film.
2. His ability to derive generalizations from the experience.

Lesson Approach:

Through the story of Abraham Lincoln, we have discussed how Abraham Lincoln walked several miles to return a few pennies that belonged to someone else. We have discussed what satisfactions he received from being a very honest individual. Today, through a short film, we will look at another approach to honesty.

Lesson Development:

A. Film description (Not to be given to pupils.)

Film: *The Dollar Bill* (3 minutes)

A young boy has been given a grocery list and several one dollar bills. After leaving his house, he reads through the grocery list and counts his dollar bills. The boy places the list and money in his pocket and in doing so he drops one dollar bill. A second boy comes upon the scene and finds the one dollar bill. The film should be stopped at this vital point, and the problem becomes a matter of group discussion or one child may analyze what he would do in this situation.

The film poses two different approaches to the problem. Within the film three key questions are given. These questions may be placed on the chalkboard.

Key Questions:

1. What will he do with the found money?
2. What would you do?
3. Why would you do it?

B. Show film without comment.

C. Follow-through discussion (First direct attention to the last two of the above questions):

1. What would you do if you found some money and you did not see anyone lose it?
2. To what extent must one go to get money or a lost article to the proper owner?
3. What do you think of the saying, "Losers weepers, finders keepers?"

D. Weighing alternatives:

In view of our analysis, what policy should one follow when finding a lost item or money?

E. Example solutions:

1. Return the item or lost money to the individual you see lose it.
2. If you do not know to whom it belongs, advertise in the paper.
3. Take the lost money or item to the police station and seek their help in finding the owner.

Discuss advantages and disadvantages of each solution as it is posed.

F. Deriving generalizations: (Suggestive only)
1. Honesty is a good policy to follow.
2. Ideals of honesty can be goals for which to strive.

It is evident from the foregoing lesson illustration that the film was used as a means of bringing human interest into a problem situation. Dramatic play or even class discussion could have been used with possibly the same effectiveness. However, the film had the advantage of economy of time and a carefully staged setting, specifically designed to further the lesson objective. The impact of the lesson rests with the entire experience —not just the film itself.

VALUES

Films are uniquely valuable for creating a carefully staged setting.
Films create an advantage of economy of time.
An educational film can present different sides of a story. It can present the normal along with the spectacular.
Films can contribute to critical thinking.
Educational films can relate content materials in textbooks to life experiences.

LIMITATIONS AND PROBLEMS

Films have been widely misused. When using films, a decision must be reached relative to its probable effectiveness as compared with other available modes of instruction.
Films have the disadvantage of being costly to rent or buy.
Availability and scheduling are always a problem with films. Alternate activities must be planned in case the film does not arrive.
Documentaries and sponsored films do not always present a true picture of the events portrayed. There is a tendency to capture the sensational.

FILM ANALYSIS ILLUSTRATIONS

I. Useful in the science area (middle grades)

    Unit: Conservation

    Concept: Man, animal, and plant life all depend upon one another.

    Problem: What policy should one follow concerning wildlife in the forest?

    Lesson Development:

        Film: *Patterns of the Wild* (26 minutes)
        (Sponsored Film: U.S. Department of Agriculture, Forest Service, State Fish and Game Department and the National Wildlife Federation.)

        Key Questions:

        1. Why can't all animals survive in the forest?
        2. How does one harvest the forest in the area of timber and wildlife?
        3. Why does forest life depend upon death?

II. Useful in the social studies area (upper grades)

    Unit: The Presidents of the United States

    Concept: World events shape the destiny of man.

    Problem: What world events and preparation made it possible for Dwight D. Eisenhower to become President of the United States?

    Lesson Development:

        Film: *A Place in History* (28 minutes)
        (Documentary Film: National Archives, General Service Administration, Washington, D.C.)

        Key Questions:

        1. Why did World War I change Eisenhower's life?
        2. What events of World War II placed Eisenhower in a leadership position?
        3. What human qualities did Eisenhower have that endeared him with the people of the world?

III. Useful in the science area (elementary grades)

    Unit: Space Travel

Concept: The scientific knowledge of many people made it possible for men to walk on the moon.

Problem: What made it possible for men to walk on the moon?

Lesson Development:

  Film: *Eagle Has Landed* (30 minutes)
  (Documentary Film: National Space and Aeronautics Administration, General Services Administration, Washington, D.C.)

  Key Questions:

  1. Why was governmental action necessary in order that men might walk on the moon?
  2. What scientific preparation was necessary?
  3. Why were people of the world brought closer together because of the moon walk?

IV. Useful in the health area (primary grades)

  Unit: Foods

  Concept: The diet of bears is like that of humans in that it is unusually varied.

  Problem: Why is the diet of bears similar to that of humans?

  Lesson Development:

  Film: *Brown Bear Diet* (4 minutes)
  (Single Concept Film: Walt Disney Nature Library, Ealing Films, Cambridge, Mass.)

  Key Questions:

  1. What protection does the brown bear have against bees when gathering honey?
  2. How does the diet of the brown bear compare with that of humans?

16

REVIEW METHOD

The term "review" is almost as ambiguous as class discussion. Teachers speak of reviewing *for* a test, reviewing the *results* of a test, reviewing important words or terms, reviewing the major points of a lesson, and so on. Too often a review is little more than repetitive practice or drill. While there is a definite place for such practice, when drill is *substituted* for review the results *must* be disappointing. Review, literally, means a re-view or a re-look at something. Thus review might be better called a new view, that is, a view of some problem from a new angle. It is a technique of guiding the pupil in the application of original learnings to related situations.

FUNDAMENTAL PROPERTIES

In addition to enhancing transfer of learning to related life situations, review may contribute substantially to the permanence of that which is learned. Unlike class discussion which focuses attention to one particular problem, review emphasizes the recognition of many, related problems. Its widespread misuse reflects a general misunderstanding of the essential properties involved.

Initial Learning Requirements

Before an individual can take a *re*-view of a situation, he must have viewed it at least once before. There is a tendency to assume

173

adequate initial learning when the pupil has read his text or is able to verbalize answers to factual questions. Thus one loses sight of the basic nature of the learning process—that of coping with basic educational *problems*. The products of each educational experience consist essentially of centralized ideas, generalizations or concepts. These, in turn, become the necessary data for review lessons. If previous experiences have emphasized the acquisition of knowledge only, it is logical (but fallacious) to conceive review as a mere repetition of these facts. Generalizations *must* be derived prior to effective review.

Recall

Recall is a fundamental aspect of review. Basic unit generalizations are brought together in one lesson for the first time. By recalling some of the methods and techniques employed during the original learning experience, the learner may develop associations which will enhance his recall of basic ideas. Although some clarification of generalizations is often necessary, the primary objective is to bring the ideas together for further analysis.

Extending Associations

Once basic, previously derived, generalizations have been brought before the group, their application to related problems is emphasized. Although specific lesson generalizations, like facts, may not apply readily to broad problems, it is relatively easy to combine them into broader concepts for this purpose. Review is most effective when generalizations are somewhat comparable in scope to unit concepts. (See Chapter 1, Gaining the Concept.) They are most effectively utilized, however, when pupils themselves derive the concepts. Processes of reflective thought reach their peak as pupils identify related problems to which previous learnings apply.

REVIEW PROCEDURE

Review is common; it can occur incidentally at any point within a lesson, or it can be the major portion of a lesson. Yet, most authorities suggest that teachers as a whole cannot, or at least do not, make adequate applications of the procedure. Burton,[1] for instance, states that he has seen several hundred reviews in progress, but practically none that amounted to anything more than drill. Why the difficulty? Is it because the technique is unusually difficult? (This does not seem likely.) Or is it due more to an incomplete understanding of the procedure involved?

Although it is recognized that a *re*-view or *re*-look is important at any point during a lesson, the emphasis in this chapter is on review lessons which occur at the culmination of a unit or block of work. The basic essentials can be readily applied to other review situations.

Recalling Basic Unit Generalizations

Each lesson should be culminated with from one to five pupil-derived generalizations. Collectively these generalizations embody a major lesson concept upon which the lesson rests. In a review lesson, pupils are expected to recall most of the generalizations derived during the unit. There is a natural tendency to expand specific lesson generalizations into broader concepts. This process should be encouraged. To illustrate from an art lesson concerned with Color Relationships:

Lesson generalizations:
1. Light, bright colors evoke a happy, gay mood.
2. Dark, somber colors generally evoke a depressing mood.
3. Different colors have different emotional impacts. (Red, for example, is happy, exciting.)
4. Colors symbolize ideas. (Blue, for instance, is associated with loyalty and honesty.)

In recalling these generalizations, pupils might be encouraged to evolve the following concept: Color may be used to create mood and symbolize ideas. In this manner the major unit concepts (usually four or six) are clarified and written out for the benefit of the entire group of children.

Recalling Generalizations

Basic unit concepts are related to other problems through a skillful process of questioning. The objective is to help pupils realize the

[1] William H. Burton, *Guidance of Learning Activities*, 3rd ed. (New York: Appleton-Century-Crofts, Inc., 1962), p. 460.

wide applicability of that which has been learned. The process often is initiated by asking questions of advocacy. Such questions usually begin with the word "Should." An advocacy question directs attention to one particular solution to a problem. Sometimes "How" or "Could" questions are useful in this respect. To illustrate from an art lesson, Color Relationships: "Should (*or* How could) we use color to improve our homes?" Possible responses might include the following:

1. Bright-colored walls would make the room gay.
2. Light colors in a small room would make it look larger.
3. Dark colors may be used to make a large barnlike room appear smaller.

Each suggested application is discussed briefly for the purpose of clarifying the idea. No effort is made to resolve issues in a review lesson, as the function is merely that of *recognizing related problems for expansion of knowledge.* (In some instances, of course, such problems may reveal the need for further consideration of basic issues. In such cases, other appropriate techniques will be employed.)

In a review lesson, pupils should assist in recall of basic generalizations and derivation of concepts; they should bear the major responsibility for extending these learnings to related areas. It may be necessary for the teacher to offer a few suggestions as a means of preparing pupils for further analysis. There is a decided tendency to rush pupils through a review lesson, assuming that most of the important relationships are obvious. The evidence quite clearly suggests that pupils transfer learnings only to the extent to which they are taught to transfer. Several hours might be profitably devoted to such activities.

Evaluating the Experience

An appropriate review generates considerable enthusiasm and creativity. When individuals begin to understand how their school experiences can be applied to out-of-school problems, they tend to develop and maintain a high degree of interest. Such behaviors will be apparent in other class activities as well. The teacher himself also will become more conscious of the importance of transfer of learnings to related situations.

The review lesson, designed to extend learnings to related problems, is closely akin to evaluational experiences. Test items, for example, serve a similar purpose. However, test item situations must include problems other than those introduced during reviews. The purpose is to determine if the individual can make such associations and relationships on his own.

PLANNING FOR REVIEW

A major factor contributing to poor review lessons is inadequate planning. Teachers quite naturally are interested in clarifying facts and principles; they are less interested in extending these. Yet, it is through extension and association of ideas that adequate understanding is best revealed. The illustrated plan represents that review which is usually introduced at the culmination of a unit.

LESSON PLAN ILLUSTRATION (art area—middle grades)

Unit: Drawing

Concept: Will involve all the unit concepts as an essential aspect of the lesson.

Problem: How can we relate what we have learned about drawing to different situations?

Goals: After this lesson, the pupil should have furthered his understanding of the basic principles of drawing, as evidenced by:

1. His ability to identify related problems in class review
2. His ability to apply basic principles to related problems
3. His ability to draw parallels with problems previously studied

Lesson Approach:

During the past two weeks, we have emphasized the principles of drawing and we have pointed out how drawing can be an important tool of education. We have seen that drawing is a very important aspect in our world. Today, we will take a look at some of the areas where drawing can be used to solve problems.

Lesson Development:

I. *Analysis of the previous unit experiences:*
   What generalizations or big ideas evolved during our study of this unit?

    A. Quantities can be compared through drawings.

    B. Relationships can be shown through drawings.

       1. Organization charts can show relationships.

       2. Comparison drawings can show relationships.

    C. Drawings can be used as attention-getting devices.

    D. Ideas can be expressed through drawing.

II. *Recalling how the major concepts were derived:*

    A. Each child created a drawing to depict quantities or amounts. Stick figures were used to represent people. Coins were drawn to represent money, etc.

    B. Each pupil executed two drawings expressing (1) organization relationships and (2) comparison or contrasts.

    C. To illustrate an attention-getting device, each child made a drawing to move the observer to action.

    D. Each child made comic-strip type drawings to express an idea.

III. *Extending unit concepts to related problems:*

With our ideas before us, let us briefly consider other areas to which they may apply. For example:

    A. Should we use drawing to improve arithmetic?

       1. Drawings can show proportion.

       2. Percentages can be shown through drawings.

       3. Circle graphs could be used in arithmetic.

    B. Might we use drawings to improve business?

       1. As attention-getting devices drawings could be used to advertise what businessmen want to sell.

       2. Drawings can be used to tell people who can not read what the businessmen want to tell them.

    C. How could we use drawings to improve oral reporting?

       1. Drawings attract the attention of those listening.

       2. Drawings can be used to condense ideas.

       3. Drawings can show comparisons, contrasts, and relationships to help people understand the presentation.

    D. Could we use drawings to improve communication?

       1. Expression can be shown through drawing.

       2. Drawings can clarify meaning.

       3. Drawing can evoke interest.

IV. *Deriving Generalizations:*

From our treatment of related problems, what big ideas seem to stand out?

A. Drawings are capable of improving every area of the curriculum in school.
B. Drawings can be utilized to improve many areas in our world outside of school activities.

VALUES

Review is uniquely valuable for facilitating application or transfer of learnings to related situations. It has long been recognized by psychologists that individuals apply or transfer learnings to new experiences to the extent that they are taught to make this transfer. Review is designed for this purpose.

The formulation of new associations and relationships, through review, renders learning more permanent; forgetting is reduced.

Review enables the teacher to correct misconceptions and misunderstandings which inevitably arise in group learning situations.

Review procedures are extremely flexible. They may range from the informal five minute review to extended reviews of several hours. This flexibility feature has sometimes worked as a disadvantage, especially when review sessions have been ill-conceived and inadequately planned.

LIMITATIONS AND PROBLEMS

Review has been widely misused. Often mistaken for review are recitation sessions in which the learner has been expected to recall specific facts for a test.

Prior to initial learning, review is a waste of time. To make a *re*-view of learning not thoroughly understood in the first place results in chaos.

Review is deceptively easy. Even when review is used for the purpose of expanding learning, it is extremely easy to get bogged down on some related issue. If this occurs, review purposes may be impossible to achieve.

Review is extremely difficult to conduct. The major factor contributing to poor reviews is inadequate planning.

ILLUSTRATED REVIEW PROBLEMS

I.   Useful in the physical education area (upper grades)

Unit: Teamwork in Sports

Problem: How can we relate what we have learned about teamwork to our lives?

Unit Concepts:

1. We are on teams all our lives.
2. Each player has a responsibility to the team.
3. It is important to bring others into team participation.

Extending concepts to related areas:

1. How may teamwork be used in research groups in the
classroom?
2. How can we use teamwork in girl scouts or boy scouts?
3. How might we use teamwork principles in our family?

II. Useful in the language arts area (primary grades)

Unit: Discussion Techniques

Problem: How can we relate what we have learned about discussion techniques to everyday situations?

Unit Concepts:

1. Speak on the question or subject being discussed.
2. Explain ideas so they are easily understood.
3. Tell only one fact or idea at a time.
4. Make explanations simple by avoiding too much detail.

Extending concepts to related areas:

1. Is it possible to use discussion techniques in other school
activities?
2. How could discussion techniques be used at home?

III. Useful in the social studies area (middle grades)

Unit: Interdependence of States

Problem: How can we relate what we have learned about interdependence of states to practical aspects of living?

Unit Concepts:

1. People in our state depend upon services, products, and
food from other states.
2. Our state exports minerals and products to other states.
3. People of all states depend upon one another.

Extending concepts to related areas:

1. Is it possible to find interdependence in our homes?
2. How may it be possible to have such a variety of food to eat, clothes to wear, and products to buy?
3. How can we use the principle of interdependence in our classroom?

IV. Useful in the science area (middle grades)

Unit: Machines

Problem: How can we relate what we have learned about machines to other situations?

Unit Concepts:

1. A machine is anything that makes "work" easier or transfers a force.
2. A machine can gain either force or speed (distance), but not both at the same time.
3. Six simple machines make up all compound machines.

Extending concepts to related areas:

1. How might machines be used in your home?
2. How can simple machines help you if you were lost and without modern conveniences?
3. Is it possible that simple machines might be used in future inventions?

17

TEACHING OUTSIDE THE
CLASSROOM OR FIELD TRIPS

At some time many pupils and teachers have been involved in a field trip or excursion. It has been a part of almost every teacher's schedule, but all too often the learning experiences inherent in such an outing are not fully explored or planned. Many times such a trip may be seen by the pupil as a holiday from school and by the teacher as a series of management difficulties with thirty children. Through adequate preplanning, however, a field trip or excursion can be an invaluable learning experience for all.

FUNDAMENTAL PROPERTIES

The quality of any field trip rests upon a number of basic properties; for instance, it makes it possible for the child to expand his learning environment. The constrictive qualities of the school building and classrooms for a learning environment are well known; therefore, through field trips the child's learning milieu is greatly expanded. Other fundamental or basic properties necessary for field trips are the organizational patterns, relatedness to ongoing classroom activities, point of interest, and socializing skills.

Organizational Patterns

Two basic organizational patterns may be used in field trips —teacher-directed and pupil-directed.

Teacher-Directed. In the teacher-directed field trip, the teacher selects the problem, directs the pupils in observing and collecting the data, and assigns the children responsibilities for reporting aspects of the outing.

Some advantages of the teacher-directed organizational pattern are that more detailed observations are made, trial and error is eliminated, and an efficiency of time is achieved. The teacher can introduce more concepts to children in a teacher-directed excursion than in a pupil-directed outing.

Many disadvantages also are apparent. The range of observation for the children is limited by the teacher's ability to select items for discovery. Also in a teacher-directed field trip there is little opportunity for the pupil to select relevant material or reject irrelevant information.

Pupil-Directed. The teacher's role in a pupil-directed organizational pattern for field trips is to establish the location and date for the excursion. Also he would motivate the pupils and prepare them for the learning experience as well as be involved in the follow-up activities.

The pupils would clarify the tasks to be done on the field trip as well as plan how they might communicate their findings to the class following the excursion. The pupils would plan how they might solve the problems posed on the field trip.

The advantages of this approach are many, for instance it provides for *maximum application of creative thinking and problem solving* among the children. The pupils also may pursue areas that interest them. The pupil-directed pattern of organization makes it possible for the pupils to be involved in all areas of *problem solving.*

Some possible disadvantages could be the level of maturity of the children who are doing the planning and the ability of the group to make adequate plans. Depending upon the grade level of the children and the problem to be studied, modifications could be made in the organizational pattern from the teacher-directed organizational pattern at one end of the continuum to the pupil-directed organizational pattern at the other end with many levels in between.

Relatedness to Ongoing Activities

If field trips are to be important and valuable to the children, the excursions should be *planned in relation to ongoing unit activities.* Field trips can be a means of enriching the children's study by taking them to a learning situation which is not easily visualized through reading or discussion. Some field trips may be taken near the beginning of the unit for gathering information on specific topics or problems. Other field trips may be taken during the unit so that the pupils may get new motives or different directions for their studies. A field trip may be taken at the end of a unit as a culminating activity. Whenever the field trip is taken, it should be related to the classroom activities and unit requirements.

Point of Interest

A central point of interest is a necessary ingredient for a successful field trip. No matter where the excursion may be, it is important that the trip *meet the needs of the children* involved and be of interest to them.

For younger children a short trip may be made to the fire station, police station, school nurse's office, dairy, local museum, library, park, and other similar places. For older children the field trip could be to an assembly plant, factory, planetarium, newspaper office, national forest, and other places where more complex activities may be observed.

Socializing Skills

Many different values are achieved from field trips aside from gathering facts and observing first-hand activities. To some children, the many activities engaged in as they work together and socialize with one another are important values. Therefore, a fundamental property of field trips is the socialization that takes place among the children as they discuss, write about the activity, sit together on the bus or ask questions of the guide. This too is an important aspect of a field trip; however, this alone is *not* an adequate purpose for a field trip.

FIELD TRIP PROCEDURES

An effective field trip or excursion involves far *more than the actual outing*. Careful preplanning, establishing problems to solve, evaluating the outing, and deriving generalizations from the data gathered are all essential procedures for an effective field trip. The procedures outlined in this section are included to assist the teacher in planning an effective field trip.

Problem Identification

After the teacher has clearly identified the basic concept(s) to be taught, he selects an instructional method or technique which seems most appropriate for concept attainment. The field trip method is especially useful in that the guide can present to the children a sequentially planned series of field experiences which will lead to the development of one or several concepts. Generally, the basic concept(s) is first approached through textbooks or other reference materials. It is then extended and applied to the learner's own life through the excursion. To illustrate from the science area—A study of living things suggests: Living things are in constant change. From this basic concept children on an outdoor field trip could be asked to find as many examples as they can showing change in living things.

Preplanning

Children must be *involved in planning* the trip if it is to be successful. This planning must include developing the purpose for the trip; when, where, and how to make the excursion; and follow-up activities. Children in the upper grades can take more responsibility in the preplanning stages; however, it is obvious that primary grade children may need much more direction. Nonetheless, *all* children at *any* grade level should be involved in some of the planning.

Transportation may be necessary for some excursions. The school bus usually is the preferred transportation because of insurance regulations and liability laws. If the bus tour is lengthy, plans should be made to occupy children's time while traveling. Valuable learning and language arts experience may be accomplished while riding on the bus. For example, children may keep a log of their trip complete with departure time, weather conditions, road conditions, points of interest enroute, and such other items as they wish to include.

Several weeks prior to leaving on the field trip it is necessary to communicate with the people at the place of visitation so that they will be available for guide service or permission to visit will be acknowledged. Often it is appropriate for the teacher to make a personal tour of the place for visitation to determine exactly the nature of the trip and to determine in advance any problems that might arise when the children arrive. Not only should guide service be considered in the preplanning stage, but restroom facilities and food services must be considered too.

Parental written consent is a necessary prerequisite for a child to participate in most trips. If parents understand the nature and purpose for the field trip there should be no problem in securing permission.

In the preplanning stage not only should the children discuss the forthcoming excursion, but some pre-reading on the subject is also necessary. Concepts and purposes should be developed so that the *children know exactly* what they are *looking* for on the tour.

The Visitation

For a field trip to be successful, the children must be able to become directly involved in what is to be seen or heard. It may be necessary to divide the children into smaller groups. If this is necessary then several guides may be required and the children will see the same things but at different times.

If questions have been sent to the guides in advance, the tour will be focused upon what the children and teacher wish to see or hear. Of course, the children will see and hear much more than might have been anticipated. Older children may want to take notes or write down some information. Smaller children may need paper bags for the collection of items while on the field trip. Paper and pencils, bags, and other necessary equipment should be made available at the visitation site.

Evaluation

After the trip and back in the classroom, an evaluation of the activity should be made. Several questions should be answered. Was the field trip a success in the sense that it fulfilled its aims, purposes, and objectives? Was the time spent from the classroom worthwhile or could as much be accomplished in the same amount of time in the classroom? How did the children feel about the excursion?

Many different forms of evaluation may be used by the teacher. Some children may wish to write a class story concerning their impressions, and other children may wish to use the tape recorder. Some pupils may wish to write a short play, design a bulletin board, set up a display, make a diorama, write a report or become involved in some other activity based on the trip.

In the evaluation, attention is directed toward the basic concept(s) that was identified to be taught. The evaluation activities should help the children to understand, to develop more clearly, and to reinforce the concepts that were identified for the field trip.

Deriving Generalizations

As a culminating activity, pupils are encouraged to derive generalizations from the field trip experience. These are basic ideas which pupils are expected to transfer to related situations. At this point, field trip evaluational materials are related back to the basic content materials and relationships are formed.

PLANNING FOR FIELD TRIPS

In addition to careful preplanning for a field trip or excursion, a lesson plan must be developed. Major emphasis will be directed to the essential steps in a lesson plan for a field trip. The illustrated plan involves a problem-solving approach.

LESSON PLAN ILLUSTRATION (kindergarten or first grade social studies area)

Problem: Why are rules, railroad signals, and signs needed at railroad crossings?

Concept: Rules, signals, and signs at railroad crossings are very important for our safety.

Goals: After this lesson, the pupil should have furthered his understanding of safety around trains and railroad tracks, including rules, signals, and crossing signs, as evidenced by:

1. His proper use of these devices during the field trip.
2. His ability to discuss the purpose and meaning of signals and crossing signs on the field trip and follow-up activity in the classroom.
3. His ability to write down the purpose under each sign.
4. His participation in writing an experience story on safety rules.

Lesson Approach:

Now that we have discussed the importance of railroad transportation to us and our country, what should we know about safety around trains? Have you ever been riding in a car and the car was stopped so a train could cross the road? What would happen if the car did not stop? Why do we need rules for crossing the railroad tracks? What do these signs and signals mean? If no signs are by the railroad tracks, what safety rules should one follow?

Signs, signals, and rules of safety around railroad tracks are very important. We need to know these rules and what the signs and signals mean so we will not be involved in an accident or get hurt.

Preplanning:

"What plans are necessary before we can take a field trip?" the teacher asks. The pupils would be guided to suggest necessary steps such as the following:

1. Where could we see these railroad signals and signs?
2. How could we get there?
3. What could we do at the railroad tracks?
4. When does the train pass by there?
5. Who could tell us about the safety rules and railroad signals and signs?
6. How can we tell our parents about an excursion?

These questions and others could be discussed in the preplanning stages. The children would be divided into groups and assigned specific tasks at this time.

Visitation:

The visitation will be made to a railroad station or depot. The guide will focus his discussion at the visitation sight upon safety rules, and the purposes for the railroad signs and signals. The children will be able to see how the signals and signs are used when trains approach. The children will demonstrate safety rules around trains and railroad tracks.

Evaluation Activities:

1. Follow-up discussion concerning the purposes of rules and signals.
2. Label each sign by giving its purpose.
3. Write an experience story concerning the field trip emphasizing safety rules and the purposes of railroad signs and signals.

Deriving Generalizations:

Why are rules, signals, and signs necessary at railroad crossings? When do we need rules, signals, and signs in school situations? Some examples might be as follows:

1. Rules are needed so everyone will know what to do at certain times.
2. Signals and signs are like punctuation marks in our writing. They direct others how to read what is written.
3. Rules help us to live better with one another.

VALUES

A field trip is realistic. The children have an opportunity to view and be a part of the real thing.

Inasmuch as the visitation makes the experience real to the child, the field trip captures the interest and imagination of the learner.

By seeing and analyzing real problems, the pupil is able to bridge the gap between school and real-life experiences.

It is possible through field trips to develop many language arts experiences.

Field trips reduce the constrictive qualities of school buildings and classrooms.

Learning situations which are not easily visualized through reading and discussion may be developed into a field trip.

LIMITATIONS AND PROBLEMS

The field trip is time-consuming. If used extensively, it will definitely limit the content material which can be covered.

Field trips may not be as successful as they might be because teachers develop inflexible habits of thinking about the teaching process involved in excursions. Many teachers may look at the field trip as thirty children clustered together receiving a lecture.

Difficulty encountered in managing and directing a group of children in a new and unfamiliar setting is a limitation of field trips.

Sometimes field trips are visualized by the children as a holiday from school. Excellent preplanning activities with the children involved in these activities should eliminate this feeling.

ILLUSTRATED FIELD TRIP PLANS

I. Useful in the science area (kindergarten or first grade)

Unit: Our Autumn World

Problem: What happens to leaves of trees and bushes and grass in the autumn?

Concept: The leaves of many trees, grass, and bushes change in autumn.

Visitation: With a child's decorated bag, take a discovery walk about the play ground or nearby neighborhood. Observe the change in leaves from trees and bushes and grass. Put samples in the bag for further activities in the classroom.

II. Useful in the social studies area (fourth or fifth grade)

Unit: Life During Colonial Days

Problem: How was life different in colonial days compared to our life today?

Concept: During the colonial period in United States history, the people had to make by hand many of the items they needed in their homes and shops.

Visitation: Museum depicting life during colonial days. The clothes worn, machines used, magazines and books read bring the child closer to visualizing the colonial period.

III. Useful in the reading area (upper grades)

Unit: Newspapers for Information

Problem: What processes are necessary to print a newspaper?

Concept: Many steps and processes are necessary in printing a newspaper.

Visitation: Newspaper plant where the newspapers are printed can help the child see the processes in printing a paper from news reporting to printed paper and newsboy.

IV. Useful in the science area (fifth or sixth grade)

Unit: Living Things in Our Environment

Problem: Do living things depend upon one another? Find evidences that they do or do *not* depend upon one another.

Concept: Living things are interdependent upon one another in our environment.

Visitation: A park or any outdoor area would provide ample opportunities for pupils to find many examples of how living things are interdependent.

V. Useful in the music area (any elementary grade)

Unit: Music Listening

Problem: How many musical numbers can you identify?

Concept: Music with which the child can identify will aid in his music listening skills.

Visitation: A young people's concert at the concert auditorium provides excellent opportunities for the children to apply good music listening skills. Music is played that appeals to them.

VI. Useful in the art area (upper grades)

Unit: Art Communicates

Problem: How do these masterpieces of art communicate?

Concept: Art is a method of communication.

Visitation: An art gallery can provide children with an opportunity to visualize how art communicates. Allow each child to determine how various art pieces communicate; then have the guide explain how he feels the various art masterpieces communicate.

18

USING GAMES AND KITS

The intellectual capacities, curiosities, and interests of our present-day pupils demand that the teacher should go beyond the traditional textbooks for learning in the classroom. Thus games and specialized learning kits are becoming another aspect of the elementary school curriculum. In the school curriculum games offer various possibilities for action in a learning style that is chiefly mental, yet it includes freedom, intuitive thinking, problem solving, and reactive responses of physical movement.

FUNDAMENTAL PROPERTIES

Games and kits embody the fundamental aspects of a pleasurable activity, which is simple in operation and involves mental, physical, and emotional activities on the part of the player-learners. Another fundamental property of the game is the competitive or non-competitive aspect the game can have as determined by the teacher.

Pleasurable

Games add fun to learning for almost everyone including elementary school children. An enjoyable way to transmit knowledge is to make a game of the subject matter under study. Because of the pleasure games give to the child, the game activity reinforces learning. Children are willing and anxious to learn tedious skill drill activities if it is in the form of a game. The game becomes pleasurable to the pupil because he is *relating to* and *with his peers*. Therefore, a fundamental property of a game or kit *must* be its pleasurable nature.

Simple

Games should be relatively simple. If the game has simplicity, it will help to build self-confidence within the pupils playing the game. Simple game activities will allow each child to compete equally with all other children in the classroom and allow enough chance in the game so that any pupil or team can win. The simplest aspects of a game will include three major parts—the players, objectives or outcomes for the game, and rules under which the play takes place.

The game activity should be compatible with the child's level of maturity. Forcing early practice or asking the child to play a complex game before his maturity level is adequate will have a deleterious effect. The game selected should be both simple and appropriate for the children that will be playing the game.

Mental

Another fundamental property of a game is that it involves mental activity on the part of each pupil. The child who is involved in a highly imaginary play situation is building readiness for analyzing, hypothesizing, and developing generalizations. Mental and creative reasoning is fostered and practiced in playing a game. The mental activity when playing a game both directly and subtly increases the child's confidence in adapting to and choosing among various alternatives. These types of mental activity lend themselves to solving problems in many areas of the elementary school curriculum.

Physical

The exercise of motor functions involved in game and play activities is a physical benefit which children acquire while playing games. In coping with problems in games the child is actively involved with his environment and the challenges of the game. He is a person who *does* and who *acts* in the game situation. Thus, the physical aspect is another fundamental property of game activity.

Emotional

Games also can be used to satisfy emotional needs. A game play activity provides for a safe release of tension or aggression which a child may feel or develop in regular school routine. Games interspersed at frequent intervals during school activities will aid the child who is tense and needs opportunities to relax. A game that will provide an emotional outlet for children is still another fundamental property to be considered.

Competition

The nature of the game implies that there may be pupils who win and pupils who lose, yet a game should be so constructed and organized that all those that play learn. If individual competition is to be minimized, group competition can be in the game plan. Self-competition can be given to children who are not as successful in the direct one-to-one competitive games. Of course, direct competition for many pupils can be highly motivating. Another approach to more evenly match children for games is to give a child who is less successful in direct competition a handicap. The handicap could be worked on points, scoring or some other method of measuring progress. Remember in the old-fashioned spelling bee, the child that needed the practice most was the first child out of the game. The competitive aspect of the game should be so organized that the child that needs the most practice gets it.

GAMES AND KITS PROCEDURES

Game activities can take many forms. It can occur informally between two individuals, or it may be organized as an activity involving opposing teams. The games can involve the entire class or they can be played in small groups. Whatever the organization for the game may be, there are certain procedures a teacher should follow. Accordingly, the game procedures are discussed below.

Identifying the Problem

In using games in the classroom, the teacher first decides his teaching objectives and the scope of the subject matter he wishes to have included in the game activity. He must identify the problem and then select a game that would help the children in understanding the concept to be taught in the game. All too often, teachers select a game to be played and *hope* the children will learn *something*. In the proper use of games the problem is identified and is taken from the ongoing classroom activities. The game should be used as an *effective teaching* device not just something to fill in the day's activities. For example, the teacher may find that during the reading lesson, children are having difficulty in the discrimination of vowel sounds. He then selects the game activity, *Vowel Lotto*, which helps children to discriminate the vowel sounds.

Game and Kit Rules

Before children begin in game activities, they need to know the rules and regulations for the game. Often many children become frustrated and unhappy because the game rules have not been fully explained. Usually it is helpful for the teacher to play the game first, then he can better explain the game to the children. With young children the game scoring activities and rules should be very simple. More mature children can be involved in elaborate games with many rules. The important element to remember in game rules is to *keep them simple* no matter what age the children may be.

Pupil Involvement

All children need to be involved in the game activities. Most educational games are designed for maximum participation by the children and very little, if any, spectator activities. A helpful way to get pupils involved might be to start a pair or group in the game activity, then divide the group and add to the two groups people who have not played the game. Dividing the groups and adding new children to the game activity can be continued until all children are involved. This technique also will help children who have difficulty in understanding the rules because the rules will be taught or at least reinforced as the children enter the group with children who already know how to play the game. Pupil involvement is an essential ingredient for game activities whereby children can *learn by doing*.

Rewards

Many games are constructed in such a way that children can *win* or, at least, reach some *reward* or *goal*. For many children the reward seems to be learning subject matter in a non-threatening activity. If the game is organized with winners and losers, even the loser has the reward of reinforcement of skills, understandings or other learning processes while playing.

VALUES

Games and kits are effective in stimulating pupil interests and involvement.
Motivation and pupil interaction in the classroom are greatly improved through the use of games.
Games are especially successful in focusing the pupil's attention on a particular set of concepts. The attention span of children is appreciably lengthened because of the excitement surrounding the playing of the game.
The immediate feedback which games provide to pupils helps the child to judge his own performance.
Games are versatile in that both the fast and slow learners can be involved simultaneously in the activity.
Many areas of the curriculum which are not otherwise demonstrable in the classroom may be presented through the use of games.

LIMITATIONS AND PROBLEMS

No formal studies offer proof that educational games are more effective
than conventional classroom procedures. Some educators feel games
should not be used in the classroom because children do not learn as
they are too busy having fun during the game activity.

In games it is often difficult to establish evaluation criteria as to what the
game is actually teaching.

Transfer of learning may be especially difficult from game situations to the
actual ongoing class activities.

Games may place more emphasis on the child winning the game than upon
learning the concepts involved in the game.

Competition which many games generate may have a bad effect upon the
slow learner.

SOURCES OF EDUCATIONAL GAMES
AND KITS

Useful in the language arts area:

1. Dean, John F. *Games Make Spelling Fun.* Belmont, California:
    Fearon Publishers, 6 Davis Drive, 1968. This book has a collection
    of graded spelling games that can be used in the classroom in
    teams and individual games.

2. Dolch, Edward W. *Dolch Readiness Materials, Dolch Sounding
    Material and Dolch Sight Material Games.* Champaign, Illinois:
    Garrard Publishing Company. These Dolch materials consist of
    the following games: Take, The Syllable Game, Group Sounding
    Game, Consonant Lotto, Vowel Lotto, What the Letters Say, Group
    Word Teaching Game, Picture Readiness Game, Who Gets It?,
    Match Games, Read and Say Verb Game.

3. Heilman, Arthur, et al., consultants. *Phonics We Use—Learning
    Games Kit.* Chicago, Illinois: Lyons and Carnahan, 407 East 25th
    Street. This phonics game kit has ten complete games to assist
    children with phonics.

4. Lamb, Pose, consultant. *Spelling Learning Games.* Chicago, Illi-
    nois: Lyons and Carnahan, 407 East 25th Street. There are five

kits of spelling games. Each kit contains five games which reinforce spelling patterns and principles.

5. Parker, Don H., and Scannell, Genevieve. *Reading Laboratory I: Word Games, Grades 1–3.* Chicago, Illinois: Science Research Associates, Inc., 259 East Erie Street. This is a game kit that provides children with phonics practice.

6. Platts, Mary E., et al. *SPICE, Suggested Activities to Motivate the Teaching of the Language Arts.* Stevensville, Michigan: Educational Service, Inc., P.O. Box 219, 1960. This book contains many suggestions for seatwork activities, games, and independent work activities for children in kindergarten through grade eight.

Useful in the arithmetic and science areas:

1. Dolch, Edward W. *Dolch Arithmetic Games.* Champaign, Illinois: Garrard Publishing Company. These Dolch arithmetic learning games consist of the following: Say-It Games (for addition, subtraction, multiplication, and division), First Arithmetic Game, The 10 Game, Pay The Cashier, and Make One.

2. Dumas, Enoch. *Arithmetic Games.* Belmont, California: Fearon Publishers, 6 Davis Drive, 1967. This book lists arithmetic games that are suitable for use with children in kindergarten through grade six.

3. Englemann, Siegfried, and Carnine, Doug. *Distar and Strategy Games.* Chicago, Illinois: Science Research Associates, Inc., 259 East Erie Street. The Distar Games reinforce skills in arithmetic. The Strategy Games provide practice in making strategy decisions. Both games are designed for groups of five to seven pupils.

4. Platts, Mary E. *PLUS, A Handbook of Activities to Motivate the Teaching of Elementary Mathematics.* Stevensville, Michigan: Educational Service, Inc., P.O. Box 209, 1964. This book contains games and activities for counting, number meaning, telling time, money, drill in basic facts, fractions, and arithmetic challenges.

5. Roy, Mary M. *PROBE, A Handbook for Teachers of Elementary Science.* Stevensville, Michigan: Educational Service, Inc., P.O. Box 219, 1960. This book has suggestions, activities, and games to aid children in science. It has materials on simple machines, flight and space, weather, earth science, light and heat, sound, electricity and magnetism, the plant, and animal kingdoms.

Useful in the social studies area:

1. Dolch, Edward W. *Know Your States Game*. Champaign, Illinois: The Garrard Press. This game helps children learn geography, spelling, sounding, and pronunciation of the states.

2. Kaplan, Alice, et al. *American History Games*. Chicago, Illinois: Science Research Associates, 259 East Erie Street. This game was developed by Abt Associates. Each of the six history games deals with major issues in our country's past. The games are Colony, Frontier, Reconstruction, Promotion, Intervention, and Development.

3. Roy, Mary M. *SPARK, A Handbook for Teachers of Elementary Social Studies*. Stevensville, Michigan: Educational Service, Inc., P.O. Box 219, 1965. This handbook has motivating suggestions and game activities for history, geography, economics, civics, community life, and culture.

Useful in the elementary school curriculum:

1. *Bibliography of All Published Material on Educational Games*. Monmouth, Oregon: Teaching Research, Oregon State System of Higher Education. This lists the known and available educational games that may be used by the classroom teacher.

2. *Educational Games*. Cambridge, Massachusetts: Abt Associates, Inc., 55 Wheeler Street. Abt Associates has developed numerous educational games for specific clients.

3. Gordon, Alice Kaplan. *Games For Growth: Educational Games in the Classroom*. Chicago, Illinois: Science Research Associates, 259 East Erie Street, 1970. This book includes descriptions of games, where to get the games, how to evaluate and design games.

4. Many games with educational value may be purchased in toy stores, school supply houses, and general merchandizing establishments. These games can be used as developed or adapted to fit the objectives established by the teacher in the classroom.

19

TESTING TECHNIQUES

Tests are designed to provide the teacher with a quantitative measure of some experience. On the other hand, the quality of a test is an assessment of the value of the quantity being measured. Since evaluation, to a substantial degree, is based upon the tests that teachers themselves produce, this chapter is designed specifically for those who desire to improve the quality of test items. It is recognized that other measurement and evaluation tools, such as rating scales, checklists, and anecdotal records, must be used in conjunction with tests.

FUNDAMENTAL PROPERTIES

The quality of any test rests upon a number of basic properties, some of which relate to the purposes being served. Some understanding of the properties, treated in this section, is essential if the teacher is to profit fully from the techniques offered in the latter portion of this chapter.

Concept Application

Learning for what? This is a basic question that every teacher must ask himself repeatedly. Teachers and pupils quite naturally become engrossed in the content details of subject matter. A mere acquisition of specific facts, however, may provide a rather poor means of assessing the usefulness of the learning experience. It has been established that pupils quickly forget specific details. They may remember basic concepts (big ideas), however, for an indefinite period of time. (Refer to Chapter 1, Gaining the Concept.) Basic concepts, then, become the fundamental ingredients for subsequent experiences. Many test items are designed to determine if such concepts can be applied appropriately in related situations.

Reflective Processes

It seems reasonable to assume that a substantial portion of school learning is based upon an orderly process of critical or reflective thinking. In short, an individual when confronted with a difficulty will assess the situation in terms of the available facts, will consider possible solutions or courses of action to take, and will finally select or act upon the solution which seems most compatible with the data available. Instructional methods are viewed as different approaches to the reflective or problem-solving situations. They may be new to the individual but involve application of definite concepts gained from the educational experience.

Validity

A valid test is one which measures what it is supposed to measure. For example, if ten major concepts have been identified and emphasized during a unit, the test must be based upon these concepts. While it is appropriate to include some items dealing with specific facts pertaining to concepts, major emphasis must be focused on the learner's ability to *use* the concepts in related situations.

Generally the number of test items pertaining to any given concept should approximate its relative emphasis during the instructional program. If several hours of instruction were given to one concept while only one hour of instruction was devoted to a second concept, three times as much test emphasis might be placed on the first concept.

Reliability

Every teacher is concerned with the trustworthiness or consistency of his test results. Does Johnny's poor mark indicate a general lack of understanding in the area, or might it merely reflect errors due to chance and poor test items? How much would his score change if the test was administered several times without the influence of his previous test experiences?

Although it is impossible to eliminate all chance error, a simple item analysis will reveal those sources of inconsistency due to poor and/or ambiguous items. An accurate index of item difficulty and discrimination can be obtained by determining how well a given item is related to success on the test as a whole. The most accurate procedure entails contrasting the responses of the highest 27 percent of the examinees with the lowest 27 percent. The procedure is long and laborious; however, it is possible to conduct an item analysis in ten to twenty minutes by using pupils. This slightly different procedure, as described by Paul B. Diederich,[1] involves separating test papers into top and bottom *halves*. Use of test *halves* renders smaller and fuzzier differences, since some papers fall into one or the other half by chance. On the other hand, the procedure has the practical value of involving *all* pupils while the analysis is being made. (The top and bottom *quarters* analysis leaves one-half of the class idle during the procedure.)

The difference between the high and low *halves* should be 10 percent, that is, 10 percent more of the top half should respond correctly to an item than those in the bottom half. In a class of thirty pupils, for example, at least three more pupils in the top half than in the bottom half should select the correct response. The minimum acceptable high-low difference of 10 percent (for halves only) is accurate for the *middle range* of item difficulty, that is, if a total of from 25 to 75 percent of the pupils make correct responses to the item. This approximation is reasonably accurate until one reaches items that fewer than 20 percent or more than 80 percent of the class answered correctly. In a class of thirty pupils the 20- to 80-percent range (for which the 10 percent discrimination difference is reasonably accurate) would fall between six and twenty-four pupils. Any difference of three or more within this range would be reasonably acceptable. As noted earlier, most items which fall outside of this range would be too hard or too easy.

By separating test papers on the basis of scores equally between the upper half and the lower half and passing them to the right half and the

---

[1] Educational Testing Service, *Short-Cut Statistics for Teacher-Made Tests*, Bulletin No. 5 (Princeton, New Jersey, 1960), p. 7.

left half of the pupils in the class, the teacher is ready to conduct his item analysis. He will want to obtain four figures for each item, labeled and defined as follows:

H = the number of "highs" who got the item correct
L = the number of "lows" who got the item correct
H + L = "SUCCESS"—total number who got the item correct
H − L = "DISCRIMINATION"—the high-low difference

As the teacher calls out the item number, he may have selected pupils count the show of hands for him and do the necessary adding and subtracting.

A teacher will soon discover that the high-low difference for some of the items will be zero or negative. This indicates that the better pupils are doing no better, or perhaps worse, on an item than the poorer pupils. An inspection of the item often will reveal the cause. Accordingly, the item can be improved prior to its use on a subsequent test. Eventually one may be able to build up quite a reservoir of *discriminating* test items.

There may be two or three items on a test which did not discriminate satisfactorily for no apparent reason. When there is time, a teacher may want to subject these to a second stage of item analysis (assuming a multiple-choice item). This may be accomplished by determining how many of the "highs" chose each response and then how many of the "lows" chose each response. Thus a response which tended to confuse the "highs" may be easily identified. Perhaps this group suspected a trap or thought it too obvious.

Objectivity

A test item is said to be objective if it is clearly stated. Most words have several meanings. Therefore, it is important for a teacher to clarify intended meanings so that pupils will understand the question in the same way. Both essay- and objective-type items run the risk of being misunderstood. The qualified essay item described later in this chapter may greatly increase objectivity. Likewise, modified multiple-choice and true-false items enable the pupil to indicate his particular frame of reference when responding to the item.

Another aspect of objectivity is associated with scoring procedure. A scoring key, which reduces the effect of personal bias, consists of a copy of the test with an indication of the acceptable responses and the various weights to be assigned to each item.

Difficulty Range

It has been established that items chosen for maximum discrimination will tend to have a difficulty value of approximately 50 percent, that is, one out of two pupils will respond incorrectly to the item. Allowing for chance clues and the like, the point of maximum discrimination usually is placed slightly higher. This assumes, of course, that each individual taking the test has the ability to comprehend the situations posed by the various items. In many classes, however, slow learners may be placed in a class with bright pupils. It is only under such conditions that item difficulty (described earlier) can be accurately assessed.

Although an item ideally will be answered correctly by 50 to 60 percent of the pupils, it may be desirable to include a few easy items (for encouragement) and a few hard items for the purpose of discriminating among top pupils. If the test is designed as a minimum essentials test, a near-perfect score may be expected of all pupils.

Time Limitations

Tests are of two types with respect to time—power and speed. A power test provides the pupil with ample time to respond to all items, whereas a speed test limits the amount of time allowed for separate sections and/or the total test time. Most teacher-made tests are designed as power tests. In attempting to include as many items as possible within a specified time limit, tests are sometimes too long for weaker pupils. Thus a power test, in effect, becomes a speed test for *some* pupils. Such a condition may produce unreliable test results.

TESTING PROCEDURES

The construction of effective tests demands careful attention to content, purpose, and level of goal achievement expected. Thus testing procedures vary considerably. Those which follow, however, should provide the teacher with a useful guide which is consistent with the other instructional strategies presented in this book.

Identifying Concepts and Goals

If the instructional process rests upon basic unit concepts (as advocated in this book), then testing procedures must be based upon such a foundation. The reader will recall that the first step in the instructional process is concept identification. Each unit concept (usually four to six per unit) provides a basis for development of unit goals, with their accompanying behavioral outcomes. As illustrated in Chapter 2, Establishing Instructional Objectives, the outcomes usually are more useful as guides to instruction than as guides to evaluation. When behavioral outcomes are first identified, the teacher is most interested in those *intermediate* behaviors which indicate progress *toward* goal achievement and concept attainment. To illustrate the point, the goal illustration used in Chapter 2 has been reproduced.

> After reading the story about an immigrant family, the pupil should further appreciate the social inequalities as evidenced by (1) his realistic *responses* in a class discussion on the problem, "What should be the United State's policy with respect to immigrant people?" (2) his willingness to examine feeling reactions resulting from a dramatic play designed to portray feelings in a specified social situation, and (3) his greater cooperation in school with children who dress differently or speak with an accent.

It will be noted that outcomes (1) and (2) are to be elicited *during* the instructional process. Although the third outcome is a *terminal* behavior, it can hardly be used for evaluational purposes in its present form.

To be most useful for evaluational purposes, behavioral outcomes must be redefined as *terminal* behaviors, and they must be much more explicit than the intermediate behaviors described in Chapter 2. The first outcome from the foregoing illustration, for example, reads: His realistic responses in a class discussion on the problem, "What should be the United State's policy with respect to immigrant people?" As a result of the class discussion, what specific outcomes might be expected? From such an experience one might expect (among other things) the learner to evaluate evidence in the area and to draw warranted conclusions from the evidence available. The unit concept, "social inequities may exist with immigrants," is used as a guide for constructing test items designed to determine how well the learner can evaluate evidence and draw warranted conclusions in the area. Likewise, the second outcome, concerned with the learner's willingness to examine feelings portrayed through a dramatic play experience, must be more specifically stated for evaluational purposes. The teacher asks himself what such an examination of feelings might produce as terminal behaviors in the pupil. Perhaps it will be increased empathy or increased skill in interpersonal relationships in the area. Test items and other evaluational tools are then constructed for assessing progress in this direction. The third outcome, although already stated as a terminal behavior, must be more specifically qualified if it is to serve for evaluational purposes. (As a terminal behavior it does not directly serve instructional purposes.) Further refinement of the outcome can be achieved by specifying the important *conditions* under which "greater cooperation with children who seem different" might be expected. For example, one condition might include the learner's willingness to accept such pupils in specific group activities. Such an outcome is probably most appropriately evaluated through direct observation.

Selecting Test Levels and Types

After the terminal behaviors for each unit concept have been explicitly identified, the teacher must decide which of these can best be examined through the use of test items. He then ascertains the level of goal achievement expected. By referring to Chapter 2 the reader will note that the cognitive domain contains six levels, the affective domain contains five, and the psychomotor domain contains four. The three domains range from the simple to the complex, and each of the lower-level objectives are necessary to the attainment of each succeeding higher-level objective. In terms of the actual instructional experience(s), the teacher decides what level of goal attainment might be expected. If, for example, oral reports were employed as the basic means of attaining a given concept, the teacher must judge how effective they were. If they were not as effective as anticipated, test items dealing with the specific concept(s) involved might be restricted to the knowledge or comprehension levels of the cognitive domain.

Identification of goal achievement level provides a sound basis for ascertaining the type of test item to be employed in each case. As indicated in the sections which follow, different test types correspond broadly to goal levels as identified in each of the three instructional domains.

Constructing Performance Test Items

For many years one of the leading controversies in the area of test construction has focused on the level of item difficulty needed to determine progress toward goals. Some teachers have assumed that a knowledge of the essential facts in given areas should be sufficient evidence of goal achievement. Others, pointing out the wide gap between knowledge and application, have suggested that more than retention is needed. Although some indication of learning can be ascertained from how well one knows the facts, most teachers would readily agree that the best indication of learning is application in natural life situations.

In many areas, especially in the area of motor and mental skills, it is relatively easy to provide test situations which demand actual life applications of the concepts involved. The illustrations which follow suggest the wide applicability of performance test items to different areas of specialization.

1. Adds fractions correctly.
2. Prepares and delivers persuasive reports effectively.
3. Recognizes plant species in the local area.
4. Summarizes effectively.
5. Selects art objects which portray a given mood.
6. Plays music according to directions.
7. Analyzes current events in terms of selected concepts gleaned from social studies.

It is evident from the foregoing illustrations that performance test items can be employed in most subject fields. In skills subjects, some tests may be entirely of the performance nature. Such items are relatively easy to construct once the desired application has been identified. The major task is to establish the conditions and criteria of acceptable performance. For example, how many plant species in the local area should a pupil be able to identify and under what conditions? How well must he speak and under what circumstances?

Constructing Situational Test Items

Unfortunately, it is not always possible to measure behavioral changes directly. In the first place, the teacher may not have an opportunity to see each pupil in a realistic situation which demands a direct application of the learning involved. Frequently the outcome will not be applied to any real-life situation for several weeks or even months, simply because the learner will not find himself in a situation demanding such application. In an effort to determine the degree of understanding, the teacher will be obliged to resort to less direct measures. In such instances he can do no better than *simulate* an experience involving an appropriate application. In other words, he builds a realistic situation which demands an application of that which has been learned. For example, in a unit on first aid, one evidence of understanding the principles involved would probably be: "He recognizes and administers first aid properly in case of shock." It is impractical to induce a case of actual shock for test purposes; however, it is possible to simulate or act out the experience. Since it is impossible objectively to evaluate such an experience for all thirty pupils in a class, a written description of a realistic situation may be as close to reality as is possible. Thus one is measured on the basis of what he would *plan* to do in the situation rather than on his *actions* in the situation. Such a procedure obviously is a compromise with what is desired, because people do not always behave the way they plan to behave. For instance, in the foregoing illustration one might describe a fully adequate plan of action, whereas in the actual situation he might become hysterical and do nothing. Despite the exceptions, however, an indication of what one *thinks* he would do in a lifelike situation is a reasonably sound prediction of what he actually would do. It is for this very reason that people plan ahead.

Multiple-choice Test Item. Learning has been described as that of resolving issues—both great and small. Testing, then, ideally would become an additional experience in the resolution of issues. The multiple-choice item can be readily adapted to the problem-solving situation. Many of man's most difficult problems involve the making of choices between known alternatives. The choices made in relatively simple problem situations often materially affect his degree of success and/or happiness in life. This is not greatly different from the problem of a pupil choosing between alternatives on a multiple-choice test item. The long test of time has convinced test constructors of the generally superior versatility and convenience of multiple-choice items. While other forms can be used effectively in special situations, the multiple-choice is more widely applicable and generally effective.

The multiple-choice question consists of an item stem and four or five responses, one of which is the best answer. The other answers are usually referred to as foils or distractors. The item stem can be in the form of a direct question or an incomplete sentence. In essence, the item stem poses the problem situation and the possible answers represent the alternative solutions. The pupil "solves" the problem by making a choice. All the foils or distractors should be plausible to those who lack the necessary understanding of the concept application involved. Some teachers include distractors which on the surface are all quite acceptable, that is, they represent accurate statements. Only one of the five possible answers is best, however, *in terms of the situation posed.* As a general frame of reference the possible answers should include one *preferred* answer; one distractor will represent a near miss; another will indicate a crude error; while the remaining distractors will tend to fall some place between those two extremes. Teachers sometimes make use of the distractors "all of these" or "none of these." These responses can be used effectively only when the question calls for a highly specific answer which is either completely correct or incorrect.

There are likely to be a number of reasons why a pupil makes an inappropriate application to a multiple-choice test item. He could misunderstand the item stem or any one of the distractors; he could interpret the question in a unique way; or he simply may not possess an adequate understanding of the concepts necessary for the application. If the first two reasons are involved, the item is not valid for *that particular individual.* Sometimes a teacher desires to achieve greater validity by giving the pupil an opportunity to qualify or otherwise justify his answer. This enables the instructor to give credit for a choice which might have been justifiably selected *from the pupil's point of view,* even though it ordinarily would have been considered incorrect. Ultimately, however, the teacher must decide whether or not the reason given is sufficient to warrant full credit for the response.

A modified situational form of the multiple-choice item is illustrated below:

> *Subject matter area:*   Social studies.
>
> *Concept:*   Pueblo Indians build homes to protect themselves from their enemies.

Item:	A. In what way was the Pueblo Indians' home like a fort?

A. In what way was the Pueblo Indians' home
   like a fort?
   1. It was made of logs.
   2. It was square.
   3. It was for protection.
   4. It was entered through a small opening.
B. Defend your answer.

If it can be assured that, during the instructional process, the teacher did not use the specific situation employed in the item, the test question demands knowledge of the facts, *in addition to* application of a basic idea (concept). Thus the pupil must "go the second mile" to respond properly to the question. The "defend your answer" part of the item serves to probe, still further, one's depth of understanding.

Essay Test Item. Like the multiple-choice item, the essay item is readily adaptable to a specific situation. Unlike other test item types, it may elicit a detailed written response. The item can involve the making of complex relationships, the selection and organization of ideas, formulation of hypotheses, the logical development of arguments, and creative expression.

The essay item is particularly vulnerable to unreliability, discussed earlier. Unlike objective items, however, it is subject to scorer unreliability. To some extent, a pupil's mark on such an item is dependent on the reader rather than on the actual quality of a response. Such weaknesses can be minimized with due precautions.

The essay item can be substantially improved if it is so constructed as to elicit an application of learnings to new or different situations. Test reliability can be improved by giving hints concerning the structure of the answer expected. Sometimes this is called the *qualified* essay question. An illustration of the *situational* essay, in which the answer is somewhat *qualified*, follows:

Subject matter area:	Social studies.
Concept:	Pueblo Indians built homes to protect themselves from their enemies.
Item:	Pueblo Indians built their homes where they were hard to find and out of reach for protection from their enemies. Discuss what the pioneers, moving West, did that was similar to the Pueblo Indians.

Scoring reliability is substantially improved by formulating an answer key in advance of marking the questions. Sometimes it is desirable to underline or otherwise call attention to key points. Pupils, likewise, may be asked to underline key phrases to call attention to important points. Scoring reliability can be increased if the pupil is not identified until *after* all items have been marked. This may be accomplished by asking him to enter his name on the back of his test paper. The practice of marking all pupils on each essay item before proceeding to the next one and completing the process without interruption may greatly enhance one's scoring consistency.

Constructing Recall Test Items

Sometimes teachers assume that if a person can recall the important facts in an area he will make actual applications when needed. Using an illustration cited earlier, one could assume that a pupil who could describe the symptoms and appropriate treatment for shock could be reasonably expected to apply that knowledge. It is assumed that the pupil will use such information to *plan* his actions and that he will *behave* according to his plans. There is considerable evidence, however, indicating a broad gap between *verbal* understanding and actual behavior experienced in the original situation.

True-False Item. True-false items have lost much of their original popularity within recent years. There are many serious limitations associated with their use. Among the most serious is a tendency for the user to emphasize isolated facts which often hold slight validity in relation to the unit objectives. Contrary to popular belief, the true-false item is so difficult to construct that it has little usefulness. This type of question tends to penalize the brighter pupil, as he is more likely to think of the exception which can alter the intended meaning. Furthermore, test makers tend to make more items true than false, to use specific determiners (all, never, entirely, and so on), and to use textbook language.

It is possible, however, to improve the true-false item substantially so that it can serve a useful function. Even if one desires to emphasize broad concepts and selection among alternatives on a test, it is quite likely that he also will desire to test for certain specific data. In such a case the true-false test item becomes quite useful. The item can be substantially improved by encouraging pupils to apply a minor concept or generalization in some way. To illustrate in the social studies area:

Concept: Pueblo Indians built their homes to protect them from their enemies.

Item: *Pueblo Indians built their homes on the plains* so they could protect themselves better from their enemies.

One of the most important means of improving the item is to use the *modified* form. Such items are designed to permit a pupil to justify or to improve an answer so that it will become a correct answer. The pupil is asked to correct all incorrect items. In order to guard against the addition or deletion of something like the word "not" as a means of correcting an item, it may be necessary to underline certain key clauses or phrases. The pupil is asked to change the underlined portion in such a manner as to make the statement correct. If change is necessary, the pupil should alter the underlined portion only. Pupils may be allowed some credit for the mere recognition of a true or false statement and additional credit for their ability to make appropriate corrections.

Completion Test Item. The completion test item also has been over-emphasized. Like the true-false item, its answer was easy to defend merely by referring the pupil to a particular page in his textbook. As a consequence, specific details and, all too often, meaningless verbalisms were emphasized. The objectives of the unit often were forgotten when tests were being constructed. The inevitable result was a tendency to gear the entire instructional process to memorizations. Pupils, likewise, realizing they would be tested in such a manner, tended to emphasize the recall of specific details and terminology. Thus cramming for tests became popular.

Despite the inherent weaknesses involved, there are occasions when the meaning of a term and the like is important enough for the inclusion of some such items. In fact, most tests will contain a limited number of these. As its name implies, the item is answered by the completion of a statement. There is an ever-present danger, however, of a statement so mutilated that the respondent is unable to understand the meaning intended. For this reason, some teachers have changed the uncompleted statement to a question form. The following example illustrates the item.

Subject matter area: Social studies.

Concept: Pueblo Indians built their homes to protect them from their enemies.

Item: Pueblo Indians built their homes in hard to find and out of reach areas for ——————.
Why did the Pueblo Indians build their homes in hard to find and out of reach areas?

——————————————————————.

Matching Test Item. Like the completion item, the matching question is of relatively minor importance. It is used when teachers desire pupils to relate such things as dates and events, terms and definitions, persons and places, or causes and events. Its chief disadvantage is that it is not very well adapted to the measurement of real understandings as opposed to rote memory. Because the separate items in the exercises should be homogeneous in nature, there is the likelihood of test clues which reduce validity. Multiple-choice items should be used whenever possible to replace the matching test item.

Appropriate use of the item is facilitated by (1) having at least five and not more than twelve responses, (2) including at least three extra choices from which responses must be chosen, and (3) using only homogeneous items or related materials in any one exercise.

Utilizing Test Results

Tests are utilized for two distinct purposes—results and process. The teacher must determine how well basic concepts can be applied in life or lifelike situations. Test results also may provide him with clues to deficiencies in the learning experiences and the need for reteaching certain concepts. Using tests as a basis for ascertaining weaknesses in the instructional process is a sound, but frequently neglected, technique.

A pupil who responds incorrectly to a given test item is, in effect, communicating evidence of a learning deficiency. By examining all items devoted to each concept, the teacher may obtain a reasonably sound basis for remedial instruction. If all or most of the group displays similar problems, special group activities may be provided. However, most deficiencies will be of an individualized nature. This necessitates individualized remedial instructional processes. Generally, each individual, utilizing his test paper as a basis, should be provided additional opportunities to make conceptual applications in areas of deficiency. Eventually this may take the form of a subsequent test, or it may merely entail informal written statements pertaining to areas of deficiency. When the teacher is satisfied that deficiencies have been corrected, at least partial credit may be allowed for the purpose of evaluation.

VALUES

When used appropriately, test items offer a sound measure of the learner's ability to apply that which has been learned.

When used for diagnostic purposes, tests are especially useful to the learner and to the teacher for identifying areas where re-learning and re-teaching are needed.

The quantitative nature of test results accommodates group evaluation. Thus test results often are more valid than results obtained through other measures.

Test items are extremely flexible. By using various types, the teacher can test for almost any level of goal attainment. This applies especially to the cognitive domain.

When used appropriately, tests can motivate the learner to greater effort. Pupils must be assured a reasonable chance of success, however. Competition with bright, or even with average, pupils for grades is self-defeating for the less able pupil.

LIMITATIONS AND PROBLEMS

Achievement on teacher-made tests is often *inappropriately* assessed in terms of all other pupils in class. Such a practice attempts to combine ability with achievement. (Standardized IQ tests are especially designed for, and accordingly are much more effective than, teacher-made tests for measuring *ability* to do schoolwork.)

Overemphasis upon competitive grades may develop an unhealthy form of competition. Competition with one's own past achievement record or competition with other equivalent subgroups is preferred.

Tests which demand mere recall or information tend to relegate learning to this level. While some items appropriately should test learnings at this level, many important class goals and instructional techniques should stress problem-solving techniques. Thus, testing devices should seek to determine progress in these areas.

Passing tests often have become the ends of education, at least in the minds of many pupils. While appropriate tests themselves should measure progress toward more basic goals, the *intent to remember and to apply* is an extremely important psychological principle.

Tests, as often used in today's schools, tend to encourage cheating and other forms of dishonesty. Also involved may be the development of some form of status order which often is closely related to community social class lines.

Evaluation, when overemphasized, tends to be made at the expense of other, more effective instructional procedures. Furthermore, the difficulty of evaluating certain basic educational goals (affective goals, for example) tends to limit the extent to which they will be taught.

ILLUSTRATED TEST ITEMS

Multiple-choice items

I. Useful in the science area

Unit: Weather

Concept: Moisture is in the air.

Item:

A. If a glass jar is filled with ice and some water and the jar is left in the classroom on a sheet of paper, which of the following would happen?

1. The paper would become dryer.
2. Nothing would happen to the paper.
3. The paper would become wet.
4. The paper would change color.

B. Support your answer.

II. Useful in the arithmetic area

Unit: Percentages

Concept: Percentages can be expressed in many different ways.

Item:

A. If the tax on your property is 4 percent of its value, which one of the following would represent the tax?

1. 40¢ per $1.00 value.
2. 40¢ per $10.00 value.

    3. 40¢ per $100.00 value.

    4. $4.00 per $1,000.00 value.

  B. Support your answer by computing a 4-percent tax for your properties which are valued at $1.00, $10.00, $100.00, and $1,000.00.

III. Useful in the social studies area

  Unit: The state of California

  Concept: Climate has always been important to Los Angeles.

  Item:

    A. In what way did the climate of California bring the movie industry to Los Angeles?

      1. The movie stars wanted good sun tans.

      2. Electric lights were too bright and caused discomfort for the movie stars so they wanted to be outside.

      3. Movie directors could depend upon sunlight for picture taking almost every day of the year.

      4. The movie people wanted to be away from movie fans on the east coast.

    B. Defend your answer.

IV. Useful in the language arts area

  Unit: Telephone Procedures and Proper Use

  Concept: A person should respect the rights of others when using the telephone.

  Item:

    A. If you are not sure of the telephone number you wish to call, what should you do?

      1. Dial the number you think is right.

      2. Ask someone else if he can remember the right number.

      3. Try several numbers hoping one will be the right number.

      4. Look up the number in the telephone directory.

    B. Give your reasons for selecting the answer you did.

Essay items

I. Useful in the physical education area

  Unit: Teamwork

  Concept: Teamwork is an excellent method for attaining goals.

Item: John and five of his classmates have been assigned the task of reporting the life of Babe Ruth. John feels the other members are not putting forth a very effective team effort. Discuss the steps that John should take to provide effective teamwork for this group.

II.   Useful in the reading area
Unit: Interpretation of Characters in Stories
Concept: Characters in a story will arouse emotional reactions on the part of each reader.
Item: After reading the book, *Lentil*, how would Lentil have felt if Old Sheep had *liked* his music?

III.   Useful in the spelling area
Unit: Studying Words for Spelling
Concept: How to study spelling words involves a definite technique.
Item: How to study spelling independently involves a definite technique. Explain each step involved in the technique.

IV.   Useful in the science area
Unit: The Plant Kingdom
Concept: Plants need three major things to make food.
Item: State in your own words what is needed for plants to make their own food.

True-false items

I.   Useful in the social studies area
Unit: Pioneer Period
Concept: Pioneers adapted themselves to their environment.
Item: In the prairie lands, pioneers built their homes out of logs because there were many trees nearby.

II.   Useful in the reading area
Unit: Phonics
Concept: A consonant blend is a combination of two or three consonant letters which are used to represent two or more consonant sounds in a series.
Item: The letters "bl" in blue are a consonant blend.

III. Useful in the language arts area

Unit: Choric Verse

Concept: The rhythm of the poem should be maintained to produce an effective choric verse.

Item: Choric verse should be done in a sing-song voice.

IV. Useful in the arithmetic area

Unit: Division Problems

Concept: To find the average of two or more numbers, add the numbers and then divide the sum by the number of items added.

Item: To find the average of 44, 33, 71, and 14, you would add all four numbers and divide by 4.

Appendix A

UNIT PLANS FOR PRIMARY GRADES

ORGANIZATIONAL UNIT

Curriculum Area: Social Studies
Organizational Unit: Transportation

Organizational Unit Concepts

1. Important services are performed by various means of transportation.
2. Safety measures should be carefully put into effect when in and around vehicles.
3. Vehicles are used to transport food, merchandise, equipment, and tools over land, water, and in the air.
4. Vehicles are constructed to transport people over the land and water as well as in the air.
5. Modern transportation has had an influence upon our lives.
6. Transportation workers have definite responsibilities in their work.
7. The family automobile performs a transportation service.
8. We depend upon transportation for many of the things we need.

Organizational Unit Introduction

Perhaps most of you are wondering about the new bulletin board which has many different pictures. Possibly some of you have had an opportunity to visit the social studies corner to see all the picture books and models there. What do each of these pictures have in common? Remember last week when Mary's father bought a new car and she told us about it? You were all interested in her new car. Here is a car in this picture. What does this car have in common with these pictures on the bulletin board? What is meant by transportation? What effect does transportation have on our lives?

Our lives are greatly affected by modern means of transportation and travel. As you look around in our room, we scarcely see any article that has not been carried at some time by rail, boat, truck, car or airplane. Transportation workers perform many services for us.

During part of this school year we will be studying all kinds of transportation. We will see how transportation really affects each one of us.

Major Teaching Units

1. Cars and Motorcycles	2 Weeks
2. Buses	2 Weeks
3. Trucks	2 Weeks
4. Trains	4 Weeks
5. Ships	3 Weeks
6. Airplanes	3 Weeks
7. Recreational Vehicles	4 Weeks

PLANNING THE TEACHING UNIT

Teaching Unit: Trains[1]

Teaching Unit Goals

1. After this unit the pupil should have an understanding of his dependence on train transportation, as evidenced by:

[1] The authors are indebted to Martha Jessup for her permission to reproduce portions of her teaching unit constructed in a course at the University of Nevada, Reno.

a. His participation in class discussion about the use of trains for transporting food, clothing, building materials, and other things necessary for life (Evaluation: Rating scale)

b. His explanation of a discussion of his city's location on a topographical map to see how far necessities must be transported to this area and geographical problems with the mountains (Evaluation: Check list)

c. His picture to be drawn of something the train transports viewing a filmstrip concerning the train (Evaluation: Direct observation)

d. His participation in the writing of an experience story concerning what trains transport to us (Evaluation: Observation)

e. His participation in the preparation of a dictionary pertaining to goods transported by trains (Evaluation: Small group interviews)

f. His participation in a discussion following a presentation of history of transportation and history of trains (Evaluation: Check list)

g. His ability to tell in his own words the story of transportation while pointing to the pictures (Evaluation: Sequence test)

2. After this unit the pupil should be able to identify the different kinds of cars on a freight train as evidenced by:

a. His participation in discussion of a freight train (Evaluation: Rating scale)

b. His ability to name the different cars when shown pictures of them (Evaluation: Individual test)

c. His ability to retell a flannel-board story which describes the cars in a freight train (Evaluation: Check list)

d. His participation in making a mural of a freight train for the bulletin board (Evaluation: Observation)

e. His ability to differentiate between the passenger cars and freight cars as he makes a train booklet (Evaluation: Sample of work and individual conference)

f. His ability to name the car or cars brought for show and tell (Evaluation: Observation)

3. After this unit, the pupil should be able to identify the different cars on a passenger train and give their purpose as evidenced by:

a. His participation in class discussion of the cars of a passenger train and the purposes of the cars (Evaluation: Rating scale)

b. His report on a train ride, real or imaginary (Evaluation: Check list)

c. His ability to name the cars of the passenger train and give their purposes when shown pictures (Evaluation: Matching)

d. His participation in the construction of a passenger train for play (Evaluation: Observation)

e. His participation in making a mural of a passenger train for a bulletin board (Evaluation: Observation)

f. His ability to differentiate between the passenger cars and freight cars as he makes a train booklet (Evaluation: Matching and sample of work)

4. After this unit, the pupil should know who works on a train and their duties as evidenced by:

a. His participation in class discussion on the train crew and its duties following a film (Evaluation: Flow of discussion chart)

b. His participation in dramatic play with the characters being the different crew members (Evaluation: Direct observation)

c. His ability to relate the facts in his own words following a film-strip on helpers of the train (Evaluation: Individual interview)

5. After this unit, the pupil should understand better what makes trains go and where they go as evidenced by:

a. His participation in a discussion of the types of trains, which would include how they move and where they run after seeing pictures which illustrate steam, oil, electric, elevated, underground (Evaluation: Check list)

b. His drawing or painting of one of the types of trains (Evaluation: Sample of work)

c. His ability to tell in his own words the outcome of an experiment on steam (Evaluation: Individual conference)

d. His ability to show on a flannel-board train where the water is put in a train and be able to relate why they need so much water (Evaluation: Direct observation)

e. His ability to discuss the importance of bridges and tunnels as observed in the train display (Evaluation: Check list)

6. After this unit, the pupil should have furthered his understanding of the safety around trains and tracks, including signals and crossing signs, as evidenced by:

a. His proper use of these devices during dramatic play (Evaluation: Observation)

b. His ability to discuss the purpose and meaning of signals and crossing signs (Evaluation: Check list)

c. His ability to draw a sign or a signal and have a caption written for him telling what it means (Evaluation: Sample of work and individual conference)

    d. His participation in writing an experience story or chart of train safety rules (Evaluation: Informal observation)

    e. His participation in dramatic play showing what might happen if there were *no* signals or signs at railroad crossings (Evaluation: Observation)

7. After this unit, the pupil should have a better understanding of the role of the ticket agent and the railroad depot as evidenced by:

    a. His ability to point out on a local map the location of the passenger and freight depots in his city (Evaluation: Direct observation)

    b. His participation in a discussion of a field trip to the two train depots (Evaluation: Check list)

    c. His drawing of a depot and his ability to describe the different segments (Evaluation: Sample of work and check list)

    d. His participation in the construction of the two depots and placement of them in the train display (Evaluation: Informal observation)

    e. His participation in dramatic play concerning the depot (Evaluation: Observation)

    f. His participation in the construction of a depot from blocks and collection of other things needed to complete the depot—ticket agent hat, red cap, passengers, accessories, baggage, tickets, money, etc. (Evaluation: Group discussion at end of period)

Teaching Unit Introduction

A brief background of land transportation will be given at the initial discussion of this unit on trains. There will be a bulletin board display showing the various modes of transportation starting with man, the burden-carrier; a donkey transporting goods; an Indian travois dragging goods; a solid-wheeled vehicle on a fixed axle; gig; stagecoach; train; and automobile. The class will be led by the teacher in a guided class discussion of the obvious reasons why the train was so important to the transportation of goods and people bringing up ideas of the size of each mode, the amount of goods each could carry, and the number of people each could carry. This should lead to our need of the train to transport goods to our city.

Further methods used to initiate the unit will be as follows:

1. A stimulating environment created by use of these materials and methods:
   a. Interesting pictures for the bulletin boards
   b. An attractive library center featuring interesting books on trains
   c. Toy trains, blocks, erector set, and tinker toys for display and play centers
   d. Many centers of interest to stimulate expression, as areas for:
      1. Wood and tools
      2. Clay
      3. Natural science
      4. Attractive games and puzzles
      5. Art
      6. Music
   e. Attractive room arrangement to include sufficient space for all activities

2. Have pupils bring in pictures, books, games, and toys pertaining to trains for show and tell period each day which will be placed in a train center consisting of a bulletin board, a table, and shelves.

3. Have records as well as tapes on trains in music-listening center.

4. The showing of a film on freight trains followed by a discussion of our field trip in two weeks to the train station and the freight yards where we will be able to see the engine and to meet an engineer.

5. Show the filmstrip "Little Toot" and play record.

6. Teach the song "Little Red Caboose." After they know the song, they will choose whether they want to be cars of the train, trees, overpass, animals along the track, stop-and-go signals or work car. The song will be sung and the children will act out their parts. If there is time, the children will change places with one another.

7. A story will be told as flannel-board characters are placed on the board. It will be told what cars are on the train, what the cars are carrying, how much nicer the trains are now than they were, and the different places trains go; ask them to pretend they are on this train as it makes its journey.

8. Make an experience chart of what they would like to know about trains *such as*:
   a. Different kinds
   b. What they carry
   c. Where trains go

    d. How trains go

    e. How fast a train goes

    f. How the train stays on the rails

    g. Whether the engineer has a hard job

9. Tell them the story of the history of trains showing the pictures in Petersham's book and a pictorial chart of the history from the 1804 steam engine to the modern diesel streamliner to the automated train of the future.

Subject Matter (Content) Outline

    Even in the space age, the power and excitement of the thundering trains are not lost on the young. The first important transportation success of the machine age, railroads remain an essential base of transportation, especially of freight. We will try to understand why a remote area like ours needs inexpensive transportation of goods both into and out of the area.

1. To find out about trains
   a. To find out the history of transportation and trains
   b. To find out about freight trains
   c. To find out about passenger trains
   d. To find out how trains go—different types
   e. To find out where trains go

2. To understand our dependence on trains for transporting goods and people
   a. To find out what trains transport
   b. To find out why trains transport goods and people

3. To know who works with trains and what they do
   a. To find out about passenger train crew and duties
   b. To find out about freight train crew and duties
   c. To find out about the railroad depot, workers, and duties

4. To understand safety methods of the trains
   a. To find out about railroad signals (how they look and what they mean)
   b. To find out about signs—what they mean
   c. To find out about safety rules for crossings, tracks, and trains

Important Concepts

1. This country is very dependent upon trains to transport goods and people long distances.
2. The passenger train cars are different from the freight train cars in many ways.
3. Many people work on both passenger and freight train crews.
4. Trains are run by steam, oil or electricity.
5. Trains run on rails overhead, underground or on the ground.
6. Signals and signs at railroad crossings are very important to our safety.
7. The ticket agent sells tickets to passengers at the depot where the train stops to let passengers on and to let baggage and goods off.
8. It is necessary to have rules, regulations, and laws.

PUPIL ACTIVITIES

I. To find out about trains

A. To find out the history of transportation and trains
1. Discuss bulletin board presentation on progress of transportation. (Goal 1)
2. Discuss chart on history of trains. (Goal 1)
3. Draw old trains at free time. (Goal 1)
4. See film: "Development of Transportation." (Goal 1)
5. See filmstrip: "History of Land Transportation." (Goal 1)

B. To find out about freight trains
1. Discuss cars on freight train and their uses. (Goal 2)
2. Name cars of freight train when shown pictures. (Goal 2)
3. Tell a flannel-board story of uses of different cars. (Goal 2)
4. Make a mural backing for their art project. (Goal 2)
5. Make the different cars of a freight train from construction paper and crayons for a booklet and room decorations. (Goal 2)
6. See two films: "The Freight Train" and "Transportation by Freight Train." (Goal 2)
7. Observe the cars of the freight trains brought for "Show and Tell" train center. (Goal 2)

8. Do matching paper on cars of freight train and passenger train. (Goal 2)
9. Set up a complete train display table with scenery and both kinds of trains. (Goals 2, 3, 4, 5, 6, and 7)
10. Take a field trip to the freight yards. (Goal 2)
11. Write an experience story and poems about trip. (Goal 2)
12. Read stories and poems about freight trains. (Goal 2)
13. Look at books on freight trains in free time or library time. (Goal 2)
14. Play with games, puzzles, and toys of freight trains. (Goal 2)
15. Draw or paint pictures of freight trains. (Goal 2)
16. Sing the song "Little Red Caboose" and act it out. (Goal 2)
17. Listen to taped story "Chuggy and the Blue Caboose." (Goal 2)
18. Listen to record "Little Engine That Could," and read along with book. (Goal 2)

C. To find out about passenger trains
1. Discuss the cars of the passenger train and their uses. (Goal 3)
2. Give a real or imaginary report on a train ride. (Goal 3)
3. Name the cars and their uses when showing pictures. (Goal 3)
4. Help construct a large passenger train for the dramatic play center. (Goal 3)
5. Help make a mural for the background of a passenger train. (Goal 3)
6. Make the cars of the passenger train for the mural and for his booklet. (Goal 3)
7. See movie: "Here Comes the Circus." (Goal 3)
8. Read stories and poems of passenger trains. (Goal 3)
9. Observe the passenger train on the train display. (Goal 3)
10. Make engine faces from paper plates. (Goal 3)
11. Retell the flannel-board story. (Goal 3)
12. Sing "Here Is a Big Train" and "Choo-Ka-Choo." (Goal 3)
13. Listen to tape: "The Little Train That Laughed." (Goal 3)

14. Write an experience story on "Riding on a Train." (Goal 3)

D. To find out how trains go
   1. Discuss pictures of types of trains. (Goal 5)
   2. Draw or paint a type of train. (Goal 5)
   3. Relate the outcome of an experiment showing how steam forms and the pressure it creates. (Goal 5)
   4. Show on a flannel-board train where the water is put in a train and why they need so much. (Goal 5)
   5. Discuss how fast a train goes; compare it to cars. (Goal 5)
   6. Show metal of which trains are made. (Goal 5)
   7. Discuss how the trains stay on the rails. (Goal 5)
   8. Listen to record, "Choo Choo Train Ride." (Goal 5)
   9. Do a finger play. (Goal 5)
   10. Play train rhythms. (Goal 5)

E. To find out where trains go
   1. Discuss importance of bridges, tunnels, and snow sheds. (Goal 5)
   2. Observe the train display, especially towns, farms, and other scenery. (Goal 5)
   3. Draw or paint a picture of a train showing the type of scenery one might see. (Goal 5)
   4. Make houses, churches, schools, and other town buildings for the display out of ½-pint milk cartons, construction paper, and crayons. (Goal 5)
   5. Make animals and people for the display from pipe cleaners and clay. (Goal 5)
   6. Make a farm from milk cartons and paper rolls for the display. (Goal 5)
   7. Put green paper down for grass, blue for lakes, make trees and shrubs from materials desired by the children. (Goal 5)
   8. Make a frieze as a background for the train display. (Goal 5)
   9. Plant grass, wheat, bird seed, rye, and oats in a shallow pan to be used as fields of grain and pasture for the train scene. (Goal 5)

II. To understand our dependence on trains for transporting goods and people

A. To find out what trains transport
1. Discuss use of trains for transporting food, clothing, building materials, cars, etc., needed for life. (Goals 1 and 2)
2. Explain the topography of the area around his city and be able to tell where mountains and valleys are on a map. (Goal 1)
3. See a filmstrip on the freight train and draw a picture of something it was transporting. (Goals 1 and 2)
4. Write an experience story concerning what trains transport to us here in our city. (Goals 1, 2, and 3)
5. Make a dictionary pertaining to goods transported by trains. (Goals 1, 2, and 3)
6. Discuss use of trains to transport people. (Goals 1 and 3)
7. Tell a flannel-board story showing what trains transport. (Goals 1, 2, and 3)
8. Teach finger plays. (Goal 1)
9. Draw and paint pictures of goods carried by train. (Goal 1)

B. To find out why trains transport goods and people
1. Discuss what might happen if no trains came through our city. (Goal 1)
2. Read stories and make up poems. (Goal 1)
3. Show flannel-board story of difference in size of buses, trucks, and trains. (Goal 1)
4. Discuss how much more a freight train could carry at one time than a bus, truck or airplane. (Goal 1)
5. Make a chart on difference in size of a train and other modes of transportation. (Goal 1)
6. Count cars on the train around our room. Some real trains have over one hundred cars. (Goal 1)
7. Discuss how much cheaper it is to send goods by train than by air. Use chalkboard for illustrations. (Goal 1)
8. Discuss how fast a train can go compared with a truck or bus. (Goal 1)

III. To know who works with trains and what they do

A. To find out about passenger train crew and their duties
1. See a film on the people who work on a train; follow up with a discussion. (Goal 4)

2. Have dramatic play using the passenger crew as characters. (Goal 4)

3. Make pipe cleaner dolls of the various passenger and crew members to put on train display table. (Goal 4)

4. Discuss why these workers are needed. (Goal 4)

5. Make chart of the workers and duties. (Goal 4)

6. Draw and paint pictures of the workers in uniforms. (Goal 4)

7. Create stories such as: "How the conductor helps the passengers." (Goal 4)

8. See a filmstrip: "Helpers on the Train." (Goal 4)

9. Discuss a meal a train chef might cook and plan to cook one of the dishes such as rice, pudding, cake, etc. (Goal 4)

10. Sing "Train" and use rhythm band instruments. (Goal 4)

11. Have dramatic play of serving meals to the passengers in the dining car. (Goal 4)

12. Listen to record: "Bugs Bunny, Railroad Engineer." (Goal 4)

B. To find out about freight train crews and their duties

1. See a film on the people who work on a train and particularly discuss the freight train crew. (Goal 4)

2. Have dramatic play using the freight crew as characters. (Goal 4)

3. Discuss why these workers are needed and what their duties are. (Goal 4)

4. Point out the right worker on pictures when his job is given. (Goal 4)

5. Make pipe cleaner dolls of the various workers for display. Could use sucker sticks or any other collage materials. (Goal 4)

6. Make chart of workers and duties. (Goal 4)

7. Draw and paint pictures of workers. (Goal 4)

8. See a filmstrip on "Helpers on the Train." (Goal 4)

9. Sing to record "Casey Jones" and then play game. (All children line up in a double line. Two are picked as engineers in the engine. They skip in a circle to the rhythm and as they come around, they choose one to get behind them as cars of the train. This goes on until all children have been chosen. When all have been chosen,

the engineers yell "Whooo Whooo" and the children scatter to their places.) (Goal 4)
10. Read stories and poems. (Goal 4)
11. Take field trip to the freight yards. (Goal 4)

C. To find out about railroad depot, workers, and duties
1. Take field trip to passenger depot and freight depot. (Goal 4)
2. Write experience story on field trip. (Goals 4 and 7)
3. Make rules concerning safety on bus, at the depots, and around the tracks. (Goal 6)
4. Have dramatic play on bus trip. (Goals 4, 6, and 7)
5. Have role-playing episode such as "Child running off from group and getting on the tracks." (Goal 4, 6, and 7)
6. Point out and mark on a local map the location of the two train depots in our area. (Goal 7)
7. Draw and paint a depot and workers. (Goal 7)
8. Show and describe the different things he had seen at the depots. (Goal 7)
9. Construct depots to be placed in the display. (Goal 7)
10. Construct a depot from blocks by the big train. (Goal 7)
11. Discuss the duties of the ticket agent. (Goal 7)
12. Discuss the duties of the other workers needed at the depot. (Red Cap, baggage man.) (Goal 7)
13. Make hats for the various helpers at the train play center, tickets, money, etc. (Goal 7)
14. Make engineer hats. (Goal 3)
15. Make baggage from cardboard, construction paper, etc. for dramatic play area. (Goal 7)
16. Read stories and poems. (Goal 7)
17. Play record and sing "Down By the Station." Actions will be used such as ringing bell, tooting horn, tooting whistle, going "clackey-clack" while shuffling in rhythm with the music. (Goal 7)
18. Count the number of men on a crew. (Goal 7)

IV. To understand safety methods of the trains

A. To find out about railroad signals
1. Construct railroad signals for the dramatic play area. (Goal 6)
2. Have dramatic play using the signals properly. (Goal 6)

3. Show picture and discuss railroad signals and what they mean and why they are so important. (Goal 6)
4. Draw or paint a signal and have a caption written explaining what it is. (Goal 6)
5. Have dramatic play showing what could happen if there were no signals. (Goal 6)
6. Observe signals on field trip. (Goal 6)
7. See film on trains and observe signals closely. (Goal 6)

B. To find out about railroad crossing signals
1. Construct railroad crossing signs for dramatic play area. (Goal 6)
2. Have dramatic play using the crossing signs correctly. (Goal 6)
3. Show picture and discuss crossing signs and why they are so important. (Goal 6)
4. Draw or paint a crossing sign and have a caption written under it, or have them do it themselves if they can. (Goal 6)
5. Observe crossing signs on field trip. (Goal 6)
6. See film on trains and closely observe crossing signs. (Goal 6)
7. Discuss the importance of cars slowing down or stopping at railroad crossings. (Goal 6)

C. To find safety rules for crossings, tracks, and trains
1. Do finger plays on safety. (Goal 6)
2. Discuss personal experiences relating to crossing railroad tracks. (Goal 6)
3. See film on safety on the tracks and discuss. (Goal 6)
4. Write poems on safety. (Goal 6)
5. Have role playing concerning someone crossing tracks on foot, in a car, and in a bus. (Goal 6)
6. Tell what they are and what they do when shown pictures of signal lights and railroad crossing signals. (Goal 6)
7. Write a chart of safety rules for crossing train tracks, such as: (1) look both ways before crossing; (2) do not run across tracks—you might fall; (3) do not cross tracks when light is red or bar is down; (4) do not walk on the tracks, and (5) do not go between trains. (Goal 6)
8. Discuss each rule thoroughly giving all things that could happen if it is not followed. (Goal 6)

9. Have dramatic play showing what could happen if there were no safety devices at the tracks or if no one paid attention to them.   (Goal 6)

PROVISION FOR INDIVIDUAL DIFFERENCES

The following guidelines will be used in this problem:

1. Adapt instruction to various levels of ability such as having the right materials and right activities for each child.
2. Have flexible plans to provide for different progress rates in learning.
3. Give special help at points of weakness in learning development such as direct teaching in weak area of those children needing assistance.
4. Encourage individual and group self-direction and initiative.
5. Enrich learning to make it significant and useful.
   a. Use of many types of related activities and learning aids.
   b. Critical thinking will be stressed.
6. Plan economy of pupil time so you will teach what they need when they are ready.

The teacher is conscious of the fact that there are individual differences so he will expect all pupils to do the following projects only:

1. Participate in classroom discussion.
2. Participate in projects.   (A variety of choices will be available.)
3. Watch flannel-board stories.
4. Watch films and filmstrips.
5. Take field trip.
6. Listen to stories and poems.
7. Sing the songs and do the rhythms.
8. Listen to tapes and records.
9. Play games.

Appendix B

UNIT PLANS FOR
FOURTH OR FIFTH GRADE

ORGANIZATIONAL UNIT

Curriculum Area: Science

Organizational Unit: Biological and Physical Sciences

Organizational Unit Concepts

1. Scientists make two types of comparison. They compare two different things under the same conditions, and they make a before and after comparison of one thing.
2. All living things adjust to change.
3. Food is necessary for growth and energy.
4. Everything in the world is made of chemicals.
5. In the case of accidents, a doctor should be seen; however, first aid can be administered until the doctor arrives.
6. Wounds and scratches should be cleaned and protected by sterile bandages.
7. Learning results in a change in behavior.
8. Wildlife management controls, manages, and uses our wildlife.
9. Water is essential for life and should not be allowed to become polluted.

10. Conservation is necessary for the earth's materials and animals.
11. Water transportation is possible because of scientific advances in many fields.
12. The earth may be the only planet that has everything we need to stay alive.

Organizational Unit Introduction

Trends in science today are quite different from just a few years ago. Science is not just for a few people; it is for all of us. In the science area we can learn facts and concepts and a method of thinking. Science is a way of solving problems in experiments and problems in living too.

How do scientists compare things? Is food (nutrition) a science? How does food help our bodies to control activities? Why worry about conserving our water, metals, and forests? These are just a few questions and problems for which we need to find the answers.

In science, as well as other areas, we need to observe accurately. Science experiments will help us to learn to observe accurately and to solve problems. After observing, we need to evaluate and use what we have learned. What we learn we can apply to our everyday lives.

This year in science we will study the world around us. We will study the physical aspects of our world, the biological aspects of our world, and human behavior. What is meant by the physical world? In studying the biological world, what do you think we might study? What is human behavior? How could we study human behavior? You can see that we will have many exciting things to study in science this year.

Major Teaching Units

1.	The Scientific Method of Comparison	3 Weeks
2.	Food Science	3 Weeks
3.	Our Body Activities	4 Weeks
4.	Human Behavior	5 Weeks
5.	Accidents	3 Weeks
6.	Wildlife Management	3 Weeks
7.	Conservation	4 Weeks

8.	Materials From the Earth	4 Weeks
9.	Water Needs	3 Weeks
10.	Drug Abuse	2 Weeks

PLANNING THE TEACHING UNIT

Teaching Unit: Conservation[1]

Teaching Unit Goals

1. After this unit the pupil will know the results of soil erosion and its effects on the land and streams as illustrated by:
   a. His ability to illustrate the types of soil erosion—sheet erosion, gully erosion, and wind erosion (Evaluation: Rating scale and test items)
   b. His ability to identify erosion damage on a field trip (Evaluation: Rating scale)
   c. His ability to report orally on an erosion problem (Evaluation: Oral report)
   d. His ability to perform experiments on how soil is made (Evaluation: Experiment and test items)
   e. His collection of different types of soil and labeling them as to composition (Evaluation: Rating scale)
   f. His discovery of living things in soil (Evaluation: Check list)

2. After this unit, the pupil will realize the interrelation of soil and water conservation as illustrated by:
   a. His performance of experiments on the ability of certain soils to retain water (Evaluation: Group work check list)
   b. His demonstration of capillary action working in the soil (Evaluation: Group work check list)
   c. His preparation of an exhibit on how crop and mulch cover prevents soil erosion by water (Evaluation: Group work check list)
   d. His preparation of a bulletin board on the effects of contouring (Evaluation: Group work check list)

[1] The authors are indebted to Margaret Hill for her permission to reproduce portions of her teaching unit constructed in a course at the University of Nevada.

   e. His recognition of the effects of water on soil on a field trip (Evaluation: Rating scale)

3. After this unit the pupil will realize the importance of forest and wildlife conservation as illustrated by:
   a. His drawing of comparative maps of the forest in 1620 and the forest in 1970 (Evaluation: Check list)
   b. His collection of pictures of important forest products (Evaluation: Rating scale and test items)
   c. His drawing of one illustration of the "Balance of Nature" (Evaluation: Rating scale and essay test items)

4. After this unit the pupil will come to a realization of the damage pollution is doing to our water and air as illustrated by:
   a. His construction of an anti-pollution poster (Evaluation: Rating scale)
   b. His report to the class on a case of pollution in our town (Evaluation: Oral report)
   c. His recognition of water and air pollution on a field trip (Evaluation: Rating scale)

5. After this unit the pupil should realize that the future prosperity of all individuals, communities, states, and nations depends on the wise conservation of natural resources as illustrated by:
   a. His participation in a guided class discussion on the problem, "How can we as a group and as individuals help conserve our natural resources?" (Evaluation: Written summary)
   b. His ability to trace back to natural resources three things he uses each day (Evaluation: Illustrated oral report)
   c. His ability to explain ecology in his own words (Evaluation: Written essay)
   d. His ability to identify specific reasons for the conservation of specific resources (Evaluation: Written essay)
   e. His collection of newspaper and magazine items about the current efforts to get better conservation and pollution laws (Evaluation: Check list)

Teaching Unit Introduction

   The first white men landed on our continent and were filled with awe because of the vast forests which covered our land. But they were not too awed to cut them down, which they did. They literally slaughtered our forest. For three centuries, three hundred years, little was done toward trying to conserve any of our natural resources. For while the forests were slaughtered so was the soil. It was improperly farmed and fertilized, it was often abandoned and left to erosion as the people moved on westward. At its best, the mining of minerals was crude and much waste was dumped wherever it was convenient, often clogging streams and rivers and polluting them.

By the close of the 1800's, we could go no further West. The forest did not stretch on forever and land, good farming, and ranching land became more scarce. So, in 1891 the National Forest System was started and the conservation movement got underway on a nation-wide scale. But the start was very slow. Not until fifteen years later was the U.S. Department of Agriculture formed. This marked the start of real conservation policy. Still, it was to take a disaster that displaced thousands of people before the government recognized a true need for soil conservation. The disaster started slowly about 1930. The great plains of our country had some dry years. By 1935, vast acreages of once-bountiful grassland lay in waste, looking much like desert sand dunes blowing in the wind. Elsewhere either drought parched the land or rainwater ran wildly off tilled fields and washed good topsoil into streams, filling them to overflowing. Lowland was flooded regularly and gully erosion was a common sight. Much of our agricultural land was in a critical state. It was then, in 1935, that Congress created the Soil Conservation Service as an agency in the Department of Agriculture. Its job was to work with the people of our land to stop the tragic and costly waste of land and water resources. Now the people were aware of conservation and, during the years between 1930 and 1950, much was done to stop the ravaging of our forests by lumbering and fire, and the ruining of the soil and water by poor farming and mining practices. By 1950, people began to relax. Much destroyed farm land had been reclaimed. The lumbering industries had programs of reforestation and the public was being more careful with fire. Dams were built to stop flooding.

Now a new crisis hit our water and air—people and industry. Too much industrial waste and sewage was being put into streams, rivers, and lakes killing the fish and ruining vegetation on their banks. Lake Erie, one of the largest lakes in the world, has few if any fish living in it and it is unsafe to swim in. Too much waste was put into the air by factories and cars creating smog over even our smaller cities. The air over New York City is so impure that it leaves the same amount of residues in your lungs each day as smoking a pack and a half of cigarettes. But like the conservation issues that came before it, we are doing too little and it may be too late. The pollution problem has been with us twenty years. Legislative laws that tried honestly to do something about it have been passed only in the last five years. Still, nothing is really being done yet on a large scale to stop pollution and nearly nothing has been done to correct existing damage.

Subject Matter (Content) Outline

1. Soil conservation
   a. What soil is
   b. Layers of soil
   c. Relationship of soil to rocks
   d. Water in soil
   e. Minerals in soil
   f. Air in soil
   g. Living things in soil
   h. Saving soil

2. Water conservation
   a. Water distribution
   b. Saving our fresh water

3. Forest conservation
   a. Forest distribution
   b. Enemies of trees
   c. Trees for everyone

4. Wildlife conservation
   a. Animals that are extinct
   b. Balance in nature
   c. Restoring the balance of nature

5. Mineral conservation
   a. Mineral distribution
   b. Mining procedures

6. Air pollution
   a. Sources of air pollution
   b. New pollution laws

7. Conservation related to ecology in the interrelationship of everything in our world

Important Concepts

1. Soil is a mixture of rocks and organic matter.
2. The earth's cover of soil consists of layers.
3. Rocks wear away and become part of the soil.
4. Plants take water and minerals from the water.
5. Earthworms turn the soil and make it arable.
6. The erosion of wind and water carries away topsoil.
7. Topsoil is protected through soil conservation practices.
8. Water is a natural resource.
9. Although water covers 70 percent of the earth's surface, it is not evenly distributed—some areas have a water shortage.
10. The wise use of forests is closely related to the wise use of soil and water.
11. Trees are used for food, shelter, and clothing—they are important to us in many ways.
12. Insects, fires, and wasteful lumbering are a threat to our forest.
13. Various animals have disappeared from the earth.
14. Animals should be protected—they help to maintain the balance of nature.
15. Minerals are non-renewable resources.
16. Minerals are not evenly distributed on the surface of the earth; we must use them wisely.
17. Air is a natural resource and it is being polluted.

Pupil Activities

1. *Collateral Readings.* The pupil will read at least two of the following booklets to supplement textbook reading. (Goal 5)

2. *Written Reports.* The purpose of the following written reports are for the pupil to learn to express himself more clearly in written language.
   a. The pupil will write his own definition of ecology. (Goal 5)
   b. The pupil will write why he thinks one particular resource ought to be conserved. (Goal 5)

3. *Oral Reports.* The purpose of the following reports are to help the pupil share his information with the class.
   a. The pupil will report orally on a specific erosion problem. (Goal 1)

    b. The pupil will report orally on evidence he finds of air and water pollution in our area. (Goal 4)

    c. Orally, the pupil will trace back to a natural resource three things he uses each day. (Goal 5)

4. *Assignments.*

    a. Find life of some kind in the soil at home. (Goal 1)

    b. Prepare an exhibit on how mulch and crop cover prevents soil erosion by water. (Goal 2)

    c. Prepare a bulletin board on contour plowing. (Goal 2)

    d. Construct comparative United States maps on forests in 1620 and 1970. (Goal 3)

    e. Prepare a collection of pictures of forest products. (Goal 3)

    f. Illustrate an instance of the "Balance of Nature." (Goal 3)

    g. Construct an anti-pollution poster. (Goal 5)

    h. Collect current newspaper and magazine items on efforts to get better conservation and pollution laws. (Goal 5)

5. *Guided Class Discussion.* This activity is designed to develop group agreement through talk and reflective thinking.

    a. One possible problem the children may resolve this way as a culminating activity could be, "How can we as a group and as individuals help conserve our natural resources?" (Goal 5)

6. *Class Discussion.* This activity will help the pupils clarify issues and search for answers on the topics studied in class.

    a. One topic that might be discussed is, "What is ecology?" (Goal 5)

7. *Teacher-Pupil Planning.* The purpose of this activity is to give the pupils practice in democratic planning and the execution of instructional activities.

    a. One possible teacher-pupil planned activity could be a cooperatively planned field trip to see good and/or bad conservation and pollution practices. (Goals 1, 2, 3, 4, and 5)

8. *Films.* The purpose of a film is to bring the material closer to real life situations. (These films are from the Washoe County A–V Catalog.)

    a. Show "Nature's Half Acre" in color, fifty minutes long. (Goal 5)

    b. Show together: "Your Friend, the Forest"; "Your Friend, the Soil"; "Your Friend, the Water." Each is in color and eleven minutes long. (Goals 1, 2, 3, and 4)

9. *35mm Filmstrips.* The purpose of a filmstrip is to clarify points. The following may be shown if the need arises:
   a. Our Land and Its Water
   b. Story of Rivers
   c. Story of Underground Water
   d. Soil Resources
   e. Work of Ground Water
   f. Work of Running Water
   g. Work of Snow and Ice
   h. Work of Wind
   i. Conserving Our Natural Resources Series
      1) What Conservation is
      2) Saving Our Soil
      3) Enough Water for Everyone
      4) Improving Our Grasslands
      5) Using Our Forest Wisely
      6) Giving Our Wildlife a Chance
      7) Using Our Minerals Wisely

10. *Experiments.* The purpose of an experiment is to give the pupil a knowledge of scientific procedure and a chance to "see for himself" the way things happen. The following experiments will be done by groups of children as demonstrations:
   a. How is soil made artificially? (Goal 1)
   b. What is the water retention of different soils? (Goal 2)
   c. How does capillary action work in soil? (Goal 2)

11. *Informal Lectures.* The purpose is to use lectures to plan work, to help clarify certain topics, and to answer questions. Topics that may need clarification with lectures are:
   a. Air pollution (Goal 4)
   b. Water pollution (Goal 4)
   c. Ecology (Goal 5)

Provision for Individual Differences

The teacher, conscious of the fact that there are individual differences, will expect all pupils to do the following projects only:

1. Read textbook assignments.
2. Read two supplementary pamphlets or fifty pages from a book or books.

3. Participate in one group work project.
4. Participate in both general class discussions and guided class discussions.
5. Participate in the cooperative planning of the field trip.
6. Complete one oral or one written report.

Those desiring to do additional or different work will be asked to read collateral readings, participate in more than one group work project, and complete an additional report on an area of conservation.

Appendix C

UNIT PLANS FOR UPPER GRADES

ORGANIZATIONAL UNIT

Curriculum Area: Social Studies
Organizational Unit: People and Nations Beyond the
American Continents

Organizational Unit Concepts

1. People and nations beyond the American continents have cultures that are different when compared to our culture.
2. The standards of living vary among people and nations beyond the American continents.
3. People from nations other than the American nations have made contributions to our heritage and our way of life.
4. There are many ways that people from other nations are similar to the people in the United States.
5. There are many ways that people from other nations are different from people in the United States.
6. Many likenesses and differences exist among the nations that are beyond the American continents.
7. Geographical location has influenced the history and cultures of people and nations beyond the American continents.

Organizational Unit Introduction

As we study these people this year, we will learn that their way of life is made up of many things. Their way of life is the language they speak and the way they write it. It is their homes and places of worship, their schools, libraries, museums, hospitals, theaters, and parks. Their way of life is also made up of their villages, towns, and cities, and their transportation and communication networks. It is the foods they eat, and even how they eat them. Their way of life is also the work they do and how they spend their leisure time. It is also their heritage of ideals and values that guide their daily living, the freedoms they cherish, and the laws they have. Their way of life—their culture—is all this and more. In social studies this year we will have an opportunity to examine these wonderful people and learn of cultures that are similar and different from ours.

This year you will learn how people are living in regions of nations beyond the Americas. You will discover that people live in different ways in various places. But you will also find that there are many similarities among people the world over.

Major Teaching Units

1.	Viewing the World	3 Weeks
2.	In Europe	6 Weeks
3.	In the Soviet Union	4 Weeks
4.	In the Middle East and North Africa	2 Weeks
5.	In Africa South-of the Sahara	2 Weeks
6.	In Japan and Korea	3 Weeks
7.	In China	3 Weeks
8.	In South Asia	3 Weeks
9.	In Southeast Asia	2 Weeks
10.	In the Island World	3 Weeks
11.	Working Together	4 Weeks

PLANNING THE TEACHING UNIT

Teaching Unit: In the Soviet Union[1]

Teaching Unit Goals

1. After this unit the pupil should have furthered his understanding concerning the world's largest country, as evidenced by:
   a. His location of the U.S.S.R. on maps and globes (Evaluation: Test items)
   b. His measurement of the air distances across Russia and relation of this to time and distance study which involves problem solving (Evaluation: Test items)
   c. His construction of the U.S.S.R. map and superimposition of the fifty states of America over the Russian map (Evaluation: Rating scale by teacher)

2. After this unit the pupil should have furthered his understanding concerning the Russian people and culture, as evidenced by:
   a. His correspondence with various agencies for information concerning the Russian people (Evaluation: Research paper)
   b. His collection of magazine articles and pictures that portray the Russian people and culture (Evaluation: Oral report)
   c. His collection of actual Russian objects to display for the class. (Evaluation: Rating scale by teacher and test items)
   d. His ability to write a short article about the Russian people (Evaluation: Written report)
   e. His participation in tasting caviar and other Russian foods to understand different foods in Russia (Evaluation: Check list)
   f. His participation in class discussion after watching movies on Russian people (Evaluation: Rating scale by teacher and test items)
   g. His participation in listening to Russian music for comparison with U.S. music and identification of musical scores (Evaluation: Check list and test items)
   h. His ability to figure the cost of consumer goods (cars, clothes, etc.) in terms of days or hours worked as compared with costs in U.S.A. (Evaluation: Test items)

[1] The writers are indebted to Jerry W. Miller for his permission to reproduce portions of his teaching unit constructed in a course at the University of Nevada, Reno.

3. After this unit the pupil should have developed a familiarization with the climate, resources, geography, and industry of Russia, as evidenced by:
    a. His location of the five geographic divisions of the U.S.S.R. (Evaluation: Rating scale by teacher and test items)
    b. His maintenance of a record of local temperatures related to U.S.S.R. temperatures (Evaluation: Analysis report)
    c. His report about one type of industry within the U.S.S.R. (Evaluation: Written report)
    d. His ability to fill in natural resources by symbols on a map of Russia (Evaluation: Check list)

4. After this unit the pupil should be familiar with the type of government and the historical events that brought about this type of government, as evidenced by:
    a. His ability to relate the revolt in Russia to the Communist Party (Evaluation: Reading analysis report and test items)
    b. His review of the factors and causes of the Communist revolt with czarist Russia (Evaluation: Test items)
    c. His participation on a panel discussion: "What should be the policy of the United States toward the Communist countries?" (Evaluation: Check list)
    d. His ability to compare the democratic system of government to the Russian system (Evaluation: Written report)

Teaching Unit Introduction

The Soviet Union is the largest country in the world. Its population exceeds two hundred million people, most of whom live in western Russia. The U.S.S.R. has many resources which include timber, farmland, iron, coal, and oil. The people are attempting to develop these resources to their fullest.

Traditionally its people have settled along its rivers which run north and south and have for centuries provided the only means of transportation. Even the Viking traders used these rivers. They traveled into this great primitive country to trade and some of them stayed as protectors and eventually became the rulers and noblemen. They were called "Russ," hence the name Russia.

Russia has had a long history of oppression. The Mongolians overran most of Asia, including Russia, in the thirteenth century. For about 240 years their cruel rule existed. Finally, in 1480, some strong Russian leaders emerged—beginning with Ivan III—and overthrew these conquerors.

The first Czar was Ivan IV (The Terrible). His rule began in 1533, and in 1547 he declared himself Czar. Ivan IV was followed by others, each taking "Czar" as title, including Peter the Great who reigned from 1689 to 1725. He was responsible for bringing western culture to Russia. He was the first ruler to leave the homeland and he traveled in Europe studying shipbuilding and navigation and absorbing the culture of the countries he visited. Upon his return, he began construction of Russia's new capital on the Baltic Sea, St. Petersburg (now Leningrad). After Peter's death, Moscow became Russia's capital city.

The long reign of the Romanov family began in 1613 with Michael and ended in 1917 with Nicholas II, the last Czar. Nicholas was removed by open revolt which led to a period of trouble and confusion. During this period of trouble and confusion the Communist Party, under the leadership of Lenin, seized control of the government and forcefully instituted their own reforms. Sweeping changes began to take place almost immediately— they seized industry, they collectivized farming, and they set up controls upon education.

In spite of all the promises and predictions by the small group of Communist Party members, the Russian people were not any better off than they were under the reign of the Czars.

World War II saw Russia unprepared and in need of help as Nazi Germany overran parts of the large country. Eventually, with the massive assistance of the United States, the intruders were pushed back out of Russia as the Soviets continued to get stronger. As the war ended additional troubles developed between the Communist Bloc countries and the western powers. These problems continued, even growing, until Stalin's death, at which time the tensions began to ease. Since then tension has generally continued to decrease.

Subject Matter (Content) Outline

While discussing this unit we will try to understand this largest country, its people, and its culture. We will try to familiarize ourselves with information concerning the climate, resources, geography, and industry in the U.S.S.R. We will try to see the differences between our way of life and the Russian way of life.

I. From Baltic to Pacific
   a. Reading the maps
   b. Exploring Asiatic U.S.S.R.
   c. European U.S.S.R.
   d. Moscow—the capital

II. Living under the Communist rulers
   a. Past history and revolt
   b. Farming the collective way
   c. Pre-collective farming
   d. Day to day in the city
   e. Longing for freedom

Important Concepts

1. Our form of government in the U.S.A. is different from the Russian form of government.
2. We, as Americans, have many personal freedoms.
3. The type of government we have is designed to preserve our freedom.
4. Human rights, human dignity, and the need to preserve these, at whatever costs, are very important to human beings.
5. Many changes were brought about by modern transportation in Russia.
6. Progress is important, but only with consideration for human resources.

Pupil Activities

1. *Letter Writing.* In advance of the actual beginning of this unit on the Soviet Union, the proper form for a letter will be exhibited on the chalkboard. The class will then jointly compose a letter, or letters, to agencies that can furnish information on the U.S.S.R. (Goal 2: The pupil should have furthered his understanding concerning the Russian people.)

2. *Oral Reports.* Each pupil will collect magazine articles and pictures that portray the Russian people and culture. Each pupil will have an opportunity to report orally on these items as well as any object of Russian origin. These items are to be placed on display

in order to generate class interest; taken one by one the items can be used to evaluate present class knowledge on the subject as well as giving opportunity to open areas of study. (Goal 2: See above.)

3. *Collateral Readings.* The pupil is expected to read at least twenty-five pages from any one or more of the following books. The purpose of the assignment is to supplement the material in the textbook. (Goal 2: See above.)

> Dawson, Grace S., *Your World and Mine* (Boston: Ginn and Company, 1965).
>
> Dolch, Edward W. and Marguerite P., *Stories from Old Russia* (Champaign, Ill.: Garrard Publishing Co., 1964).
>
> Geis, Darlene, *Let's Travel in the Soviet Union* (Chicago: Children's Press, 1964).
>
> Parker, Dr. Fan, *The Russian Alphabet Book* (New York: Coward-McCann, 1961).
>
> Ponsot, Marie (translator), ill. by Benvenuti, *Russian Fairy Tales* (New York: Golden Press, 1961).
>
> Thayer, Charles W. and the Editors of *Life*, Life World Library, *Russia* (New York: Time, Inc., 1969).

4. *Written Reports.*
   a. Each pupil is required to prepare a short article about the Russian people. The purpose is to give the pupil experience in expressing himself in a clear, precise, and understandable manner. (Goal 2: See above.)
   b. Each pupil is to write letters to various travel agencies and ask for materials which he will then use to prepare a research paper. (Goal 2: See above.)
   c. Each pupil will write a short report on a particular industry within the U.S.S.R. (Goal 3: The pupil should develop a familiarization with the climate, resources, geography, and *industry* of Russia.)
   d. Each pupil will make a comparison of the democratic system of government with the Russian government. (Goal 4: The pupil should be familiar with the type of government and the historical events that brought about this type of government.)

5. *Films.* The purpose of showing films is to stimulate interest on the part of the pupils and permit them to associate what they have learned in class with real-life situations. (Goal 1: The student should have furthered his understanding of the world's largest country; Goal 3: The pupil should develop a familiarization with

the climate, resources, geography, and industry of Russia; Goal 4: See above.)

a. Show film entitled, "Russia."
b. Show film entitled, "Russian Life Today—Inside the Soviet Union."
c. Show film entitled, "Russia and the World Today."

6. *Recordings.* The purpose of playing the records is to give each pupil an opportunity to listen to Russian music for comparison with music here in the United States and to be able to identify certain Russian musical scores.

a. Peter Ilyich Tchaikowsky's *1812 Overture*
b. Standard School Broadcast, Program 24, *St. Petersburg, 1960–61*
c. #FH5420, *History of the Soviet Union in Ballad and Song* (Russian Language)

7. *Class Discussion.* This activity will be the mainstay of classroom activities throughout this unit. This method of teaching may help pupils search for answers and topics to be discussed in the class. A good topic for classroom discussion is, "How can we better communicate to the Russian people details of our way of life?" (Goal 2: See above.)

8. *Panel Discussion.* The purpose is to stimulate each one's thinking and improve one's ability to express himself before a group. The panel will discuss, "What should be the trade policy of the United States toward the Communist countries?" (Goal 4: See above.)

9. *Assignments.*

a. Construct a map of the U.S.S.R. and superimpose the fifty states of the United States over the Russian map. (Goal 1: See above.)
b. Bring to class articles and pictures that portray the Russian people. (Goal 2: See above.)
c. Bring to class objects of Russian origin to display for the class. (Goal 2: See above.)
d. Construct a map of Russia showing the location of natural resources in this country. (Goal 3: See above.)

10. *Informal Lectures.* Informal lectures will be used throughout the unit to clarify concepts which are not adequately developed in the textbook or supplementary materials. Example: "The Major Revolt in Russia." (Goal 4: See above.)

Provision for Individual Differences

The teacher is conscious of the fact that there are individual differences so he will expect all pupils to do the following projects only:

1. Participate in classroom discussion.
2. Complete written and oral reports.
3. Read textbook assignments.
4. Do workbook assignments.
5. Participate in class projects.

Those desiring to do additional or different work will be asked to read collateral readings and report orally or in writing on an historical development of Russia that is of particular interest to them.

INDEX